BETWEEN THE WORD AND THE WORLD

ANNA MACDONALD is a writer and bookseller based in Melbourne, Australia, and a masthead contributor to the Splice literary review. She has also reviewed for *3AM Magazine* and the *Sydney Review of Books*, and writes regularly for the *Australian Book Review*.

First published in paperback in 2019 by Splice,
54 George Street, Innerleithen EH44 6LJ.

Paperback Edition: ISBN 978-1-9161730-2-6

BETWEEN THE WORD AND THE WORLD

Anna MacDonald

For Ali

The third dimension, the solidity of the chair,
the body, the tree, is, at least as far as our senses
are concerned, the very proof of our existence.

It constitutes the difference between
the word and the world.

John Berger

I

THERE'S A STORY ABOUT Iain Sinclair's shoes, and it goes something like this. Let's say, for the sake of convenience, that we're in Hackney. Sinclair attends a party where he's introduced to a woman who also doesn't know him. I imagine there are pleasantries, those how-do-you-dos and nice-to-meet-yous, those words we throw so casually away as if they don't matter. As if they weren't coordinates according to which we navigate the world and find our place within it. Regardless, pleasantries aside, there must be a pause in their conversation. There must be a pause because, Sinclair tells us, the woman looks down at his shoes. Is she struggling for something to say? I don't think so. I think she's enjoying herself. I think she's looking and thinking. I think she's taking her time, to see. Because, having looked at Sinclair's shoes—shoes made for walking, shoes that are weathered, scuffed, well-worn, having clearly covered a lot of ground—the woman looks up again, and says: "You must be a writer."

I no longer remember where I first read this story, nor when I began to notice that Sinclair returns to it repeatedly. But I do remember my first ecstatic discovery of Sinclair's writing and the moment I recognised that by reading words I was also encountering a world beyond the page. It was in the mid-2000s and I had borrowed a library copy of *Lights Out for the Territory: 9 Excursions in the Secret History of London*. The pages were dense with signs left behind by earlier readers: a coffee stain here, a dog ear there, underlinings and marginalia everywhere. Other people had passed this way before me and their lingering traces encouraged an appropriately palimpsestic reading. The book's opening essay documents an excursion intended to "cut a crude V into the sprawl of the city... from Hackney to Greenwich Hill... along the River Lea to Chingford Mount." "Walking," Sinclair writes in those pages,

> is the best way to explore and exploit the city; the changes, shifts, breaks in the cloud helmet, movement of light on water. Drifting purposefully is the recommended mode, tramping asphalted earth in alert reverie, allowing the fiction of an underlying pattern to reveal itself. To the no-bullshit materialist this sounds suspiciously like *fin-de-siècle* decadence, a poetic of entropy—but the born-again *flâneur* is a stubborn creature, less interested in texture and fabric, eavesdropping on philosophical conversation pieces, than in noticing *everything*.

I've always been a walker. Never a bookish child, I wanted to be in the world instead; I still thought of the word and the world as irreconcilably separate, then. Walking was a way of going places—to the park, down the creek, onto the street—alone or with other children (this was a time before the fear of public spaces, before organised and micro-managed "play"). As a teenager, walking helped to salve a restlessness I didn't fully understand. Less a way of going than an attempt at being still, it became a shortcut to solitude, a space to think teenage things. Later still, walking became a means of discovery, a way of deviating from the paths beaten by collective habits of movement and mind; those routes overwritten by family, friends, school. Now an adult, walking has become many things. It is a way of going places. It can be uncomfortable, boring, dully routine. Sometimes walking is still a way into solitude. But often, I do it without thinking. What I realise now—what, by walking, I have come to notice—is that at some point, I can't say exactly when, walking and reading, reading and being in the world, became one for me. I read Virginia Woolf and sought to assume the walker's "central oyster of perceptiveness, an enormous eye." I read Gaston Bachelard on space, on the elements, and especially on poetic reverie, that "triple liaison between imagination, memory and poetry," that form of "cosmic dreaming" which "positions us in a world." From Woolf and Bachelard I learned that writing is a road to dreaming the world. But from Iain Sinclair I finally, belatedly, learned to see how the worlds dreamed on and beyond the page bleed into one another. Writing and reading are, first and always, ways of being in the world. They are ways of looking and seeing and feeling and thinking, of experiencing the world in all its dimensions. Writing and reading are ways of looking and seeing and experiencing, again.

So now, looking again at the story of Sinclair's shoes, seeing it anew as I write it down, I notice that it isn't a story about shoes at all. I notice that it isn't, perhaps, even a story about Iain Sinclair. Writing it down, it looks to me rather more like a story of a woman at a party who looks and sees and thinks, who, having observed the world, makes a connection between walking and writing and then puts it into words.

II

SOON AFTER I BEGAN READING Esther Kinsky's *River*, I went out in search of a magnifying glass. Early one Sunday, I drove east to the neighbourhood of my childhood and scanned the tables of the fleamarket, sifting through the mismatched crockery and souvenir ashtrays, the rusted garden tools and mildewed terracotta pots, the war medals, postcards, biscuit tins, and children's toys. I found the magnifying glass at a stall manned by two Russians whom I took to be brothers. This was the same table where, years ago, I had salvaged a cardboard box of photographs—many of them river scenes—that spanned the decades between 1944 and 1970 and catalogued a Polish family's births, deaths, and marriages, and the houses they once called home.

The handle of the magnifying glass bears the years of another's use, but its lens is clear. With it I scanned the pages of *River*, paying particular attention to the book's photographs, following fence lines, railway embankments, deserted roads turning blindly into the distance, and wooded paths disappearing into blazes of unexpected, eerie light. I thought I was looking for clues, searching for details that were not at first apparent to the naked eye. I noted down metaphors, pursued suggestive allusions, drew connections between one thing and another, and believed I was reading *River*. But in fact, by looking closely, I was learning to see what was already there: to observe the book's "fluvial landscape," to recognise its "estuarine script," and, like the narrator, to discover a tidal universe in "the unremarkable things that lay unheeded by the wayside, things lost and not found, things left behind, unclaimed, thrown aside, things going to rack and ruin, beyond retrieval or recognition."

Kinsky is an heir to Thoreau (she has translated his work into German) and *River* is shaped by his thought in important ways. The book is an entrancing example of Thoreau's "discipline of looking always at what is to be seen." And the unnamed narrator's "slow and haphazard" walks by the River Lea, her dedication to "walking and looking" as a way of being and belonging in the world, recall Thoreau's essay 'Walking,' in which he describes this "art," best realised in sauntering, as the ability to be "equally at home everywhere."

River is a work of fiction, but I hesitate to call it a novel. It has, rather, more in common with W.G. Sebald's prose narratives which—as Kinsky's translator Iain Galbraith notes in his introduction to Sebald's poetry collection *Across the Land and the Water*—keep "at arm's length... the generic exactions (plot, character [and] dialogue) levied by the more conventional modes of writing fiction." There are similarities between Sebald's and Kinsky's prose works: the wandering narrators, the inclusion of photographs, the affective power of objects, the elemental prominence of water and fire, the emergence of memories in place, the topography of railway lines, bone mills, slaughterhouses, brickworks. These likenesses contribute to the uncanny familiarity of *River*'s narrative universe and it is due to them that I at first sought to read Kinsky's book in the way I have learned to read from Sebald: by paying attention to those strange, allusive connections from which his world is woven. But the narrative universe of *River*—while descended from Sebald's and Thoreau's—is very much Kinsky's own. In it, the narrator "looks always at what is to be seen" and, in doing so, is witness to that which has as yet gone unobserved. So it was that when I went out in search of a magnifying glass, I was also seeking another way of looking at what is to be seen.

III

THE NARRATOR OF *River* was raised on the banks of the Rhine, which, as she tells it, was "the first border I ever knew. ... It taught us what was here and where was there." Now, after living for many years in central London, she has "excised" herself from that life—"just as one might cut a figure out of a landscape or group photo"—in favour of "a provisional existence" by the Lea and an extended "leave-taking" of the city before her return to the east. Every day, from her temporary flat in London's northeast, she walks to the river and its interstitial surrounds: beyond Springfield Park and the alder grove at Horse Shoe Point to Walthamstow, Leyton, Hackney and Stratford Marshes, to Hackney Wick, Leamouth and, eventually, the Thames Estuary.

This is fertile ground, territory that has been crossed by Iain Sinclair, Rachel Lichtenstein, Gareth Rees, Will Self, and Nick Papadimitriou, among other psychogeographers, deep-topographers, and writers of place. Like Kinsky, many of these walker-writers are drawn to the liminality of the urban edge. For Sinclair, in *London Orbital*, the Lea is "a water margin" that feeds his "Hackney dreaming." In *Marshland: Dreams and Nightmares on the Edge of London*, Rees describes the Lea as carving "a border between the modern boroughs of Hackney, Leyton and Waltham Forest, and the historical counties of Middlesex and Essex." When the river bifurcates, the old Lea—for Kinsky's narrator, its "wild" arm—"plunges into Hackney Marshes, where she reconnects with a deeper chronology, before the city, before people, when monsters hunted on her banks." Here, according to Rees, the Lea "remembers herself."

The Lea is a site of myth, memory, and imagination, which in *River* is reigned over by the King: a man "conversant with grandeur, but also used to desolation," missing or deposed from his country of origin, who, "in his stark solitude," commands this enchanted area "between a landscape abandoned to all kinds of wildness, and the city." The King is witness to the rising and setting of the sun, and his ritual marks the opening and closing of Kinsky's narrative. *River* begins at twilight, when the King, encircled by ravens, faces east into the encroaching night. It ends at dawn, with "a great torrent of light" pouring over the King, the ravens and Springfield Park, "glimmering, glistening, sparkling, and finally dissolving in a blinding, golden tremor, in which all that had accompanied [the narrator] in the past months evaporated like a cloud succumbing to sunlight." Between dusk and dawn, over the course of her extended leave-taking of London, Kinsky's narrator dreams upon the "dark matter" thrown up by the river: "images [that] belonged to a past I could not even be sure was my own, touching on something whose name I must have forgotten, or possibly never knew."

It is in photographs that the narrator learns to recognise these uncannily familiar images. She carries a Polaroid camera as she walks and photographs "things that were irreconcilable with my previous life in London":

> What came to light when the developer foil was peeled from the black-and-white photo with its countless shades of grey was a memory I did not even know I had. The pictures showed something that lay behind the things the lens had focussed on, things which, for an imperceptible moment in time, the shutter release must have brushed aside. ... There was something unquestionably familiar about these landscape scenes. ... Something waved to me, whispering: Do you remember? You remember, don't you?

> from some remote depth within the white-edged surface of the photograph. And right beside it the world of the negative: nocturnal, putting a strange face on things, casting into doubt what belonged to which side, whether it was here or there, right or left.

In *River*, photographs—and Polaroid photographs especially—belong to the twilit, edgeland dreaming of the Lea. They belong to the place and time of their taking in ways that other kinds of photography do not. Because Polaroids are developed *in situ*, the narrator must take into account the weather conditions when determining how long to wait before peeling the positive image from its negative. And the "instant" nature of the Polaroid allows her to compare its subject against the photograph and its negative at once.

In their dark magic, these photographs both affirm and cast doubt upon the narrator's Rhineland river teachings: "What [is] here and where [is] there." In their "countless shades of grey," they "bring to light" the strange nocturnal world of the farther side of myth and imagination. Like the river with its "dark matter," like the found objects that the narrator gathers as she walks and with which she compiles a "barely decipherable archive of [her] homelessness," photographs remember what memory has neglected. With its "alien eye," the camera captures a "wounded landscape," just as the porcelain manufactured from slaughterhouse bones at Bow retains "a hint of rosiness" and the bricks from which London is built are repositories of "different histories," drawn from the sediment of the city's "network of countless rivers."

IV

The rivers of *River* are many—both arms of the Lea, the Thames, the St. Lawrence, the Danube, the Yarkon, the Vistula, the Oder, the Neretva, the Tisza, and the Hooghly—but they all find their source in the Rhine. In his book *Water and Dreams*, phenomenologist and champion of the elemental imagination Gaston Bachelard describes the influence of the landscapes of childhood—the environments where as children we learn to dream—upon the world we later inhabit:

> Dreaming by the river, I dedicated my imagination to water, to clear, green water, the water that makes the meadows green. I cannot sit beside a stream without falling into a profound reverie. ... It does not have to be the same stream [or] water from home. The nameless waters know all of my secrets. The same memory flows from all fountains.

Walking and looking, we learn to be at home everywhere. But this home that travels with us is forever inflected by the elemental landscapes of our childhood. Bachelard's childhood waters are tranquil, the memories they ignite are coloured by his "youthful happiness." Those of Kinsky's narrator are considerably more turbulent. For her, all rivers are border zones that conjure the "dislocation, confusion and unpredictability in a world that crave[s] order," which she first learned to recognise in her Rhineland childhood. To travel on the Rhine was to give oneself up to a "restless, transient land between two riverbanks." To live alongside it was to inhabit a world prone to floods that "washed away any sense of order", that "clawed at things that seemed fixed and inviolable," and left in its wake "dark matter for which we had no name."

Like the Rhine, the Lea marks an edge. It is just one of the between zones, border lines, no-man's-lands, gateways, and transitional spaces to which Kinsky and her narrator are drawn. These zones indicate a city's "scar lines," and for all the urban drive toward order, they are sites of lingering wildness: "terrain undescribed enough for me to apply my own names to it." Walking the Lea, taking photographs, collecting found objects, the narrator learns to look at the city in a way that had eluded her during all the years she lived there "under the delusion of belonging." Here she learns, finally, to give a name to the dark matter of her childhood river. But belonging—this calling into being—becomes possible only after the narrator leaves her London home for a place where she knows no-one and where "the street names, views, smells and faces were all unfamiliar to me." Like Thoreau's Walker Errant, having left behind family, friends, and the known world, Kinsky's narrator is now "at home everywhere." And everywhere becomes the transient world of the river, that transitional space between wildness and the city, where the water-bound cosmic reveries of childhood can, and do, live again.

The old, wild Lea "remembers herself" in the deep chronology of her marshland territory. The narrator's Lea-side walks are also journeys into memory. Along the way—"sticking to the river as if clutching a rope while balancing on a narrow footbridge"—she rediscovers "bits and pieces of [her] childhood" and finds "snippets cut from other landscapes and group photographs, unexpectedly come here to roost." Soon after arriving in the neighbourhood, the narrator discovers an alder grove at Horse Shoe Point, where curlews, lapwings, and bitterns sound their "melancholy calls," and recalls her childhood by the Rhine:

> This partly mutilated wetland wood with its childhood flowers and wild birds secretly appealing to my memory was my gateway to the lower reaches, to the path downstream that gradually taught me, during the final months of my stay, to find my own names for a city I had already spent many years labouring to decipher—names only walking and looking could force me to extract and reassemble from a web of trickling memories, a debris of stored images and sounds, a tissue of tangled words.

The allusion is clearly to a foundational trauma, which begins to be painfully extracted from a tangle of words and repressed images after the narrator passes through the gateway of a mutilated wood that distinctly recalls the sadness of her grandparents' generation. And although I am reluctant to read *River* as a Holocaust narrative—for, like Sebald, Kinsky represents the Holocaust as one in an ongoing cycle of human atrocities in which the Bosnian War receives particular emphasis—the book is indelibly marked by the horrors of the Second World War, just as the landscape through which the narrator travels is regularly marked by death.

Pre-war, inter-war, and post-war are prefixes that define the physical world of *River*, as well as the ways in which the book tells time. On her Lea-side walks, the narrator looks for traces of a past that might have survived post-war reconstruction. She travels to Croatia in search of "some kind of key to a post-war condition that refuses to be dismissed, even from the green of the grass, leaves and weeds." The memories of her Rhineland childhood are coloured as much by "the dream of the Great Straightening of the World" as they are by the river itself. And in northeast London she finds evidence of the re-ordering of the post-war world in the council flats "built on land cleared of war debris":

> The hasty cobbling together of housing in an effort to remove all trace of what lay underneath had been a major feature of my childhood. ... Buildings were constantly demolished, sites excavated and levelled, and the signs of a past that had gone awry were

> overlaid with impenetrable crusts. Disintegrating brickwork, in whose nooks and crannies the hair of former residents... still hung in rustling spider webs, was buried under the pale-grey, post-war pressed stone, permitted its return to the earth under new roads. ... Here in London the reasons for erasing traces of the past may have been different from those in the country of my childhood, but the unhappiness that inhabited the drab chasms between the houses looked remarkably similar in both.

In the country of the narrator's childhood, the removal of traces of a past "gone awry" also meant the removal of gardens that had run wild after their "unremembered owners had fled their own names." Kinsky's narrator is heir to this displacement; this loss of home, name, personal, and *placed* history. But the neighbourhood of the River Lea is home to an observant Jewish community which, during the Feast of Tabernacles, "with its rehearsed atmosphere of provisional arrangements and make-believe fragility of dwellings," celebrates "the opposite of homelessness." Here, the narrator discovers traces of the levelled past: scar lines, wounded landscapes, porcelain and bricks tinged with slaughter blood, as well as a heap of shoes sold by "the Croat" in aid of victims of the Bosnian War, "fatty soot" left over from the burning of heretics, and a canister of "broken-off gold teeth." Here, too, during her leave-taking, she discovers a provisional home.

Walking, looking, learning to see: these are the tenets of *River*. In her extended daily walks over the same territory, Kinsky's narrator adopts the "microscopic inner-eye" of Nick Papadimitriou's deep-topography. As described by Will Self, in *Psychogeography*, this is a discipline of "minutely detailed, multi-level examinations of select locales." To borrow further from Thoreau, it is an approach to place that "looks at what is to be seen," and then looks deeper. Thus, with my salvaged magnifying glass, I hoped to strip back the layers of Kinsky's photographs, and her words (staggeringly beautiful in Iain Galbraith's translation from the German), to see beyond the surface to what lay beneath. Perhaps this is the natural development of a way of looking—of learning to see—that has moved from the woods and fields of Thoreau's 'Walking' to the urban edge. But it is also the evolution of a "multi-level examination" of place that must consider what histories, myths and dreams have been built over to placate the post-war condition; what latent memories are waiting to resurface with the flood tide; what dark matter can be named by walking and looking, alone.

V

It's 2010, one of those unexpectedly mild afternoons before autumn gives way to winter, and I've spent the day reading Kristin Otto's *Yarra: A Diverting History of Melbourne's Murky River*. I put down my book as the light begins to fade, leave my flat and walk to the water's edge. After so many hours reading, I've started to muddle the worlds on and beyond the page. The oval at Como Park, where footy training is now underway, is a billabong fed by the river in wet weather. Herring Island is attached once more to the river's northern bank, as it was before the basalt quarry cut it loose. And the two boys who have settled themselves on Punt Road Jetty are lying in wait for a creature of myth.

They're sitting quietly on their campstools, these boys, a tackle box between them, the lines of their fishing rods slack and driving upriver with the current. Elbows to scabby knees, the boys bend forward over their reels. Their posture is casual, but alert. They locate the current in the course of floating leaves and other river wrack, and sink their lures alongside submerged snags they discover in the deepest water. Fingers resting lightly on their lines, each boy is intent upon the liquid vibration of his lure. Their shoulders are braced in anticipation of the lightening snap and fierce, feeding tug of the Murray cod.

These boys have heard the stories. The largest freshwater fish in Australia, one of the largest in the world. A "mighty," "beer keg," "monster" of a fish, capable of outgrowing the height of a tall man and living to be as old as one. A fish so powerful that it was once winched from the water on fencing wire secured to the rear of a Chamberlain tractor. A voracious predator rumoured to feed on anything smaller than itself: other fish, water birds and rats, possums, snakes, and, according to fishing folklore, working dogs and sheep entire. An ancient fish, as old as the Murray River itself, as old as the river's tributaries. "*The* fish," Pondi—according to the Ngarrindjeri people—that erupted from the dry earth, followed by "a great flow of water," and, with the sideways beat of his powerful tail, created the wide serpentine path of the river into which this water afterwards streamed. A fish known by scientists to have inhabited the Murray-Darling Basin for twenty-six million years and thought to have existed there, unchanged, for fifty or sixty million. A fish introduced to the Yarra River. A trophy fish—once widespread, now rare.

These boys have seen the pictures: early black and white photographs of serious men standing alongside their catch and giving it scale. More recent full-colour snaps of men grinning into the lens, crouched ankle-deep in red river clay and bent double by the weight of the fish they cradle in both arms. Flicking through fishing magazines and instruction manuals, taking note of promising locations, making lists of recommended tackle-weights and lures, the boys have studied these photographs carefully. In each instance, they have concentrated on the triumphant expression of the fisherman over the body of the fish, snapped before its muscles begin to slacken and its colours fade. Poring over these photographs, the boys magic themselves into the role of jubilant fishermen. Sitting quietly on their campstools, they trace the swollen line of the cod's creamy belly in their imaginations and prick their fingers along the sharp spines of its green-mottled dorsal fin. They bow under the weight of the dense, adrenaline-riddled body of their catch. And, later, they bend to wash their forearms and scrub the creases of their elbows where river silt and fish scales have caught in the struggle, and dried there.

Later, in January 2019, when I'm living closer to the sea than the river, and the boys stationed along the pier are fishing for snapper rather than cod, I'll see an image of another man cradling a Murray cod and bending to the water, this time to wash from his forearms blue-green algae and the scales of a one-hundred-year-old fish that has been poisoned. More than a million fish have died in one week, their bleached and bloated bodies collecting along the banks of the Darling River in New South Wales: one consequence of draining the Menindee Lakes and siphoning water away from the Murray-Darling Basin to cotton growers. It's been less than a decade, but those two scab-kneed and hopeful boys now belong to another time, and another place.

VI

SOMETIMES, I like to remind myself that we're come from water. I recall, in quick succession, that our blood is mostly composed of water, that our plasma retains the saline memory of the sea, and that drinking sea water leads first to mania, then to death. It's a complicated inheritance—water lets the weather in—but I like to feel the liquid layer beneath the skin.

Katharine Kilalea's intriguing début novel, *OK, Mr Field*, inhabits that fluid dimension, which runs within the mind and the body, and the architectural spaces built to domesticate it. Composed of serial slippages between man and machine, human and animal, order and chaos, fantasy and reality, which "dissolve the moment they [are] thought about," this is an expansive, multi-sensory narrative which at once makes manifest the human condition and upsets that condition to vertiginous effect.

The novel works against linearity and any neat interpretation of its narrative, but in précis it recounts concert pianist Mr Field's relocation, with his wife Mim, from their home in London to an imagined double of the Villa Savoye, a house designed by Swiss-French architect Le Corbusier and built between 1928 and 1931. This replica, constructed by fictional architect Jan Kallenbach and located at False Bay near Cape Town, is a "House for the Study of Water." Unlike the builders of other "Villa Savoye doppelgängers" (the black, or 'shadow,' version in Canberra, Australia, and the 'mini' version in Boston), Kallenbach "replicated Le Corbusier's [building] in all aspects apart from its location since the original

Villa Savoye overlooks the rural French landscape, while the one in Cape Town overlooked the sea." Le Corbusier intended the Villa Savoye to realise his manifesto, *Five Points Towards a New Architecture*, and, in its component parts, to embody an efficient "Machine for Living." Transplanted from Poissy to the Cape Peninsula, however, the house is cast adrift. And in it, Mr Field—whose move from London was precipitated by a rail accident following his performance of Chopin's *Raindrop Prelude*, which "had gone badly"—is likewise untethered.

Living in the House for the Study of Water is "like living on a raft." In it, according to one South African academic, "who, like a number of so-called architourists, had turned up at the house one day as though it were a museum rather than a private residence," Kallenbach failed to "synthesise" Le Corbusier's design to the local environment. Thus, the building's narrow ribbon windows, originally intended to light each room equally, instead restrict an inhabitant's view of the world, severing the ground from the sea, and the sea from the sky, and inducing a nauseating seasickness. In addition, the horizontal orientation of the house—which, according to the laws of celestial navigation, should assist Mr Field in determining his position and finding his way—undermines his known coordinates. Already undone by his unpopular performance of Chopin, his subsequent accident, and the pin that now secures the shattered bones of his left wrist and "infect[s] everything with a Gothic atmosphere," here at Cape Town, Mr Field has "lost [his] bearings" and become "unhinged."

OK, Mr Field can be read as a story of psychological disintegration, and initially I approached it as one might eavesdrop upon a therapy session. Thus the title became a casual invitation for the narrator and analysand, Mr Field, to speak. I imagined him in the "institutional" space of the House for the Study of Water, reclining on the Le Corbusier chaise where he spends so much of his time, "dredging up" memories, "brush[ing] up against... forgotten" dreams, working to repress the things he "didn't want to know," and recalling his mother, with her repeated incantation that "nobody wants to hear about your personal trials and griefs." I watched him, watching his strange double—a black dog—perform a curious *Fort/Da* game and thus rehearsing Mr Field's own fear of separation: having dropped a tennis ball at the top of a ramp, the dog's eyes "would accompany the ball's downward journey until the strain of separation became too great and he would set off after it with a scattering of legs." I listened to Mr Field, listening for the phantom Hannah Kallenbach, estranged wife of the architect whose house seemed to have "ingested some aspect of her presence," and whose spectral communications "ensure[d] that every move [Mr Field] made was tracked down and accounted for." I followed him as he followed the actual, embodied Hannah Kallenbach to her own home in Cape Town, as he crept into her garden "like a no-good animal" and looked into her yellow room which, on first sight, he felt, uncannily, was "a room [he had] known or lived in so long ago that [he had] lost all memory of it."

Mr Field has become untethered from the spatial and psychological bearings that are thought to give structure to a human world. But the exact moment—or event—of his dislocation is difficult to place. Is the uncanny, Gothic atmosphere of Mr Field's South African experience a consequence of taking up residence in the House for the Study of Water—a house that, according to Hannah Kallenbach, "was never meant to be lived in"? Or did he bring that Gothic atmosphere with him, along with the mechanical pin in his shattered wrist, and the neglected piano, which emits a "confused imploring sound" each time Mr Field passes it, and is one of the several ghosts that haunt him in Le Corbusier's machine for living?

Mr Field's undoing seems to precede his arrival in Cape Town. His initial performance of Chopin's *Raindrop Prelude* (itself a prelude to the story of his psychological disintegration) is characterised by the experience of displacement. Preparing to play, he sits still at the piano, closes his eyes and seeks "to let [the composer's] feelings [of fear, anxiety, and loneliness], by force of will, enter [his] body." Then, following this unsettling performance, when the train on which he is travelling crashes, Mr Field is "picked up [by his rescuers] and carried like a dog," enacting an elision of the human with the animal that recurs in various guises throughout the novel.

And yet, there is no doubt that it is living at the House for the Study of Water which accentuates Mr Field's condition. The novel can be read as the story of a haunted house: that genre in which psychological frailty is embodied in architectural space. Driving into False Bay (surely an indication of the trouble to come), road signs sound a warning: CAUTION! DANGER! BEWARE! Having taken up residence in the villa, Mr Field is visited by phantoms: of his wife, Mim, who even before she mysteriously disappears is a spectre in her husband's dissociative imagining ("I could see her lips moving but the glass between us cut off her voice"); of Hannah Kallenbach ("whose voice had become the background to my days"); and of "Chopin and his situation (like mine, only more lonely)."

OK, Mr Field opens with a pair of epigraphs that emphasise the relationship between architecture and the psyche. The first is from the work of philosopher Peter Sloterdijk: "A house is a three-dimensional answer to the question of how someone can be together with someone in something." It flags the novel's philosophical investigations—into love, especially—and the way that, throughout the book, every event happens in relation to something and someone else. The second epigraph, from architect Bernard Tschumi, reveals the central—doomed—conceit of building: that "[e]ach society expects architecture to reflect its ideals and domesticate its deepest fears." In the Villa Savoye, Le Corbusier aspired to reflect the ideal of an efficient, mechanised way of life. But living in Jan Kallenbach's replica, all of Mr Field's deepest fears resurface. By transplanting Le Corbusier's *système* to the Cape Peninsula, Kallenbach sought to construct a House for the Study of Water. But studying the sea, Mr Field is instead brought "up against" himself. Another of the novel's architects, Curtis Touw, plans to build a residential tower on the block alongside Mr Field's, which is intended to realise his *Manifesto for a House in the Sky*, and embody a "machine for living in together." Touw's House in the Sky begins with an orderly grid mapped over the earth but remains unfinished by the end of the novel, reminiscent of a decaying Tower of Babel, its central light shaft become a refuse tip.

What is made apparent over the course of *OK, Mr Field* is that the answer to the question of how to be in relation to others is not always the response one has looked for, and that architecture—which cannot contain the wildness of being—would do better to reflect a way of living *with* as opposed to domesticating our fears. So it is that Mr Field can begin to answer the question of how to be in relation with others—which, in this novel, is the question of how to love—only after the walls of his house have been breached and his fears allowed to surface. After the summer residents have left their seaside holiday homes, Mr Field finds himself marooned in a place that "wasn't intended for humans anymore." Storms descend upon the peninsula—"blow, blow, blow," cries the phantom Hannah Kallenbach—and work ceases on Touw's House in the Sky. Where once the regular sounds of building had kept a metronomic time for Mr Field, now the sound of rain, which has "breached the boundaries" of Kallenbach's House for the Study of Water, affords him an "enduring uniform tempo" and provides "a sense of security." Giving in to temptation, Mr Field unscrews the ribbon windows and finds the resulting feeling of vulnerability "not unpleasant." The weather has been let in, the boundaries between inside and outside dissolved, and "[t]hings were on the cusp of not being themselves."

The House for the Study of Water radically affects Mr Field's perception of the world, in calm as well as inclement weather. The ribbon windows afford him only a "partial perspective" of events, and although this partiality, with its attendant "lack of clarity," can be confusing, he finds also that it allows "room for fantasy." Likewise, the "rhyming geometries" of the house, the intersection of its different shapes ("as in a cubist painting"), and the view of the nautical horizon which makes "a person two people at once," altogether force him "to occupy several points of view," and confound his understanding of himself and others and their relation in space. There is, then, a certain catharsis to be gained from unscrewing the windows—"[i]t gave me great pleasure to be *doing something*"—and, when the wind blows in the glass, Mr Field says he discovers a "heightened receptivity in me. It made me more susceptible to the world, letting me receive its imprint directly onto myself."

Discontented by the way the windows artificially focus his perception of the world and his relation with others, Mr Field makes a revealing intervention into Kallenbach's replica of Le Corbusier's machine for living. This intervention does not mean that Mr Field's partial perspective suddenly becomes whole, but it does change his perception of one thing in relation to another: "I had the idea that it wasn't my vision deteriorating but the very glue which held the objects of the world together growing old and weak." Given his partial view and the repeated dissolution in his vision of fantasy into reality, it might be tempting to reduce Mr Field to that cornerstone of the ghost story: an unreliable narrator. But one of the remarkable aspects of Kilalea's novel is that Mr Field is, in fact, uncommonly reliable in his representation of the dislocated mind in the body in space. The glue of the world might be old and weak, fear might have breached the building intended to suppress it, but Mr Field is OK.

VII

FRIENDS OF MINE receive a commission to make a public artwork for one of Melbourne's new outer suburbs. They plan to build a ruin where the local children might play. They want their ruin to be constructed in the same style and from the same materials used to build the houses that will surround it. They want it to imagine a future and stage a history on land that has been levelled, then rigidly plotted with surveyor's pegs.

My friends meet with the suburb's architects and engineers. They want to see the designs for the new houses and to compile a list of materials so that their ruin will reflect these homes as uncannily as possible. They speak about durability; they want their ruin to last. They want it to survive the boisterous games of neighbourhood children, the cigarette stubs and broken beer bottles of restless teenagers with nowhere else to go. The architects and engineers cannot guarantee that the materials they use will last for more than twenty years.

My friends build their ruin from more durable material. They build a ruin that will outlast the new homes around it.

VIII

In the title story of his collection *Southerly*, Jorge Consiglio establishes a *mise-en-scène*—to borrow a term often used in his book—that is coloured by passionate obsession and shaped by small twists of fate, apparently insignificant details, which at first unhinge the protagonist and then clarify his destiny. All of the stories gathered in this remarkable collection belong to a world thus conceived. The universe described here is distinguished by strange doublings and the insinuation of dreams into reality. In it, each character is also another, geography determines events, and time is at once fragmented and disconcertingly continuous. This is a world in which past, present, and future are interwoven to disquieting effect.

Given Consiglio's obsession with time, it is perhaps unsurprising that he invokes a literary inheritance. In the story 'Jessica Galver,' the narrator's boyfriend, Simon, "uses Chekhov's works [and his play, *Platonov*, in particular] as if they were the hexagrams of the *I Ching*." Echoes of Stefan Zweig's *Chess* are to be found throughout the collection in recurrent references to the game, as well as the psychological and other forms of mirroring experienced by many of Consiglio's characters. But it is in 'Southerly'—a loose retelling of Jorge Luis Borges' 1944 short story 'The South'—that Consiglio most clearly claims his inheritance.

Both 'The South' and 'Southerly' open with the migration from Europe to Buenos Aires of the protagonist's grandfather. Both protagonists suffer a debilitating illness and are brought to the brink of death in the pursuit of their particular obsession: a rare edition of Gustav Weil's translation of the *Thousand and One Nights* for Borges' Juan Dahlmann, and analyses of historical chess games for Consiglio's Anatol Zakowicz. During their respective convalescences, both men travel south, which as "everyone knows," according to Dahlmann, "begins on the other side of Avenida Rivadavia." Having arrived in the south—for Anatol at the moment he crosses Rivadavia Avenue, and for Dahlmann when nearing his family home in the flatlands—each man commits himself to a violent confrontation which is, in Consiglio's words, "as necessary as it is senseless," and which instils in him a renewed sense of wellbeing.

Consiglio's retelling of 'The South' at once situates him within a narrative of literary succession and becomes a compelling example of the ways in which past, present, and future, and dream and reality, are powerfully entwined in this collection. During his long convalescence, Zakowicz has a recurring dream of Dahlmann: "It is an image: a man dressed in the style of the 1950s, who is at once himself and another, is stroking an enormous cat in a public place. The third time he has the dream he realises they are in a café on Brazil Street." In Borges' story, the episode with the cat leads Dahlmann to meditate upon the human experience of time: he "thought, while he stroked the cat's black fur, that this contact was illusory, that he and the cat were separated as though by a pane of glass, because man lives in time, in successiveness, while the magical animal lives in the present, in the eternity of the instant."

In this book the experience of time is a recurring theme, as is the juxtaposition of the human and non-human worlds. Like Dahlmann's isolation from the cat he is stroking, in Consiglio's stories a shift in the successive flow of human time can result in a man becoming "separated as though by a pane of glass" from himself as well as from the world around him. In 'Travel, Travel,' one of the most transfixing stories in *Southerly*, the protagonist, Canedo, returns to his childhood home in the Pampas to prepare it for sale. Towards the end of the story, following a meeting that "holds the key to his fate," Canedo is involved in a car accident: "The accident was a temporal discontinuity, a fracture in the progression of time." Having fallen out of successive human time, Canedo descends into a Borgesian labyrinth and discovers a reflection of himself—"as if an enormous mirror were refracting the landscape"—or as if he were seeing another, doubled world through the looking glass.

But this is only one of many shifts in the progression of time as Canedo experiences it. Over the course of the story, his temporal awareness undergoes a radical change, which culminates in the fracture described above. Initially, Canedo is a man who

> believes... that speed is the greatest virtue. ... [H]e loves technology: there's nothing faster than communications technology. He buys the latest tablets and smartphones. He's not interested in owning a status symbol, but in affirming himself in the present.

As he works on the house, however, Canedo's approach to being present through technology begins to give way. He becomes dissatisfied with technological forms of communication. His conversations with his wife, via Skype, are strangely empty, and the moment he turns on his tablet he finds that he resents his own company. In contrast, working with his hands to renovate the house "makes him real":

> He rubs his hands together, they feel gnarled, full of tendons, fibres, and blood. Canedo has transitioned from a temporary to a full life. He crossed the threshold almost without noticing. More than willpower or imagination, he has a different perception of time. He achieved this, without trying, through manual labour.

Throughout *Southerly*, Consiglio repeatedly makes connections between labour, the experience of time, and subjectivity. Some forms of work—Canedo's carpentry, for instance—deepen a character's sense of self. Others alienate workers from themselves and their free will. In 'The Running Man,' Consiglio describes men emerging from a fish meal factory thus:

> At the end of each shift, those coming out are not the same as those who entered. They've become moles. They have no eyes, their hair is straw, their skin burns or is forgotten altogether. They're dead tired. Ready for oblivion. It's normal to see them staring at their hands. They don't know what to do with their free time. While they grind fish bones they grind themselves down. They end up becoming the poorest kind of meal.

A year or so after reading this, I'll be reminded of Consiglio's factory workers, alienated from their selves, their labour, and their time, when I read the story collection *Mouthful of Birds*, by Consiglio's fellow Argentine, Samanta Schweblin. In Schweblin's story 'Olingiris,' two women—both of whom are preoccupied with fish—are ground down by institutionalised and inherently classed labour. Another fracture in the progression of time. Another doubled world seen through the looking glass. Reading Schweblin and remembering Consiglio, I will become momentarily unstuck; uncertain which side of the glass I'm reading from, and, more disturbing still, unsure if it really matters.

Technology—that "temporary" way of being present—separates Consiglio's Canedo from the world. Factory labour grinds down workers who are rendered unable to be present in their own time. But via carpentry, Canedo crosses the threshold from a "temporary"—time-dependent—life towards a full one. In 'Travel, Travel,' manual labour enables him to become "more like his true self than ever before." Importantly, it is only as this "true self" that "he inhabits the house that was his childhood."

It is no coincidence that Canedo becomes himself while working on his childhood home. In *The Poetics of Space*, Bachelard describes the house—and the childhood house, in particular—as "a psychic state." He writes of the "passionate liaison of our bodies, which do not forget, with an unforgettable house," and the ways in which "the house remodels man," including via "the nostalgia for work." From the moment of his return Canedo is literally remodelled by his childhood home: "He straightens himself up, leans on this elbows, and becomes an exact image of the bureau, the table, the six chairs and all the things that let themselves go in this place." His experience in the Pampas captures the deep connection between the past and the present, as well as the presence of the future (those meetings and events that hold the key to a character's predetermined fate). Always, in *Southerly*, these temporal connections are experienced in place.

In her book *Time*, Eva Hoffman considers the increasing deterritorialisation of temporal experience as a direct consequence of what she describes as "computer-time":

> Previous complaints about the severing of time from nature had to do with the insertion of clock time into the cycles of days and seasons. But our cognition of time is no longer even linked to the time through which we physically move. Rather, our experience of temporality is becoming increasingly deterritorialised and virtual. ... [W]hat is at stake is... the politics of experience. Our transactions with time... have profound consequences for the quality of our lives and the deep processes of subjectivity.

One way of reading Consiglio's stories is as a corrective to this deterritorialisation of temporality and experience. In *Southerly*, time and place persistently intertwine. Time moves at different rates in different places: the narrator of 'Jessica Galver' observes that "[i]n the garden the day is just beginning; but in the office it's almost midday." And Canedo's changing experience of time is directly linked to his shift away from technology towards the performance of manual labour, and the increased quality of life and subjectivity that develops as a result.

Place, in Consiglio's stories, can (and frequently does) determine temporal events. The thresholds that his characters cross are at once actual and symbolic and they have real, lived effects. Zakowicz crosses Rivadavia Avenue and enters a world of senseless violence. In 'The Terrace,' a group of teenagers meet on their school roof in a spatial and behavioural transgression that has fatal consequences. In 'The Running Man,' the narrator's slight deviation in routine leads him into a violent landscape which "candidly orchestrated the rhythm of things and determined our choices." And in 'The Night Before,' Consiglio opposes coloniser and Indigenous relations to the land in a way that emphasises the alienation of one and the belonging of the other. Here, the "landscape slowly crushes the spirit" of the invaders while an Indigenous woman looks out with "the gaze of someone used to arid landscapes, vast distances, the open sky." Place, in this collection, determines subjectivity.

But Consiglio's reterritorialisation of time and experience extends beyond character and event. Rather, temporality and territory are entwined in the material composition of his narratives. Due in part, perhaps, to his Borgesian inheritance, there is a timeless quality to Consiglio's prose, sensitively conveyed in Cherilyn Elston's lucid translation of *Southerly*. This accentuates the startling intrusion of iPads, smartphones, and tablets which immediately date the events described and which induce a sense of temporal vertigo in the reader.

Consiglio also uses shifts in tense to work against Hoffman's computer-time, according to which "time has been abstractly miniaturized to the nanosecond, and experientially reduced to the instant and the condition of immediacy." Time is elastic in these narratives—in 'Correspondence,' a story is described as having been "kneaded... as if it were a ball of clay"—and the present seems perpetually to be expanding in order to accommodate the past and anticipate the future. In 'Travel, Travel,' for instance, past actions are knit within a progressive present:

> For a week [Canedo has] been trying to scrub up the house. Every day he feels better, stronger. He observes himself in the mirror and tries to note, even down to the tiniest detail, how the physical activity is changing his body. Yesterday he started work on the pitch pine in the dining room. He removed three strips. He spent a moment tracing the grain of the wood with the tips of his fingers. He wanted to understand its logic in order to succumb to the natural order. He is obliging with the world. He tries to behave as is proper.

Such changes in tense—and this is only one of many possible examples—are disquieting in their subtlety. The final effect is a narrative deeply connected to place and time, but beneath which the ground perpetually shifts. Will Canedo come to understand the natural order of things? Or, like Borges' Dahlmann, will he be separated from the non-human world "as though by a pane of glass"? The uncertainties of *Southerly*—induced by a change in tense as in 'Travel, Travel,' or the mirroring of one character's biography in that of another, as in 'Southerly,' or the evidence that "[e]ven the most harmless detail becomes a threat" as in 'Jessica Galver'—make the experience of reading it not unlike falling through "a fracture in the progression of time."

IX

It's Federal Election Day, May 2019, and in Melbourne I'm reading Ali Smith's *Spring*. In the morning on the train going in to the bookshop where I work (when, I believe, there is still cause to hope for a change of government), I come to the part where Richard is remembering a work by Tacita Dean, a book in which she has gathered together, republished, and given "artistic attention" to the lost photographs of strangers, pictures "found in fleamarkets and junkshops." Thinking of these photographs as seen through Dean's eyes and given the attention of works of art, Richard notices that "something almost magical happen[s] to them. Whatever they'd meant to the people in them or the people who took them had disappeared. Freed from their own personal meanings, it was not just that they could be seen for themselves, but like they'd become ways to let someone looking at them see how the world really appears." I stop reading, and look up. The train carriage is full of people dressed for the football: fathers with their young sons, elderly men wearing hand-knitted beanies and scarves in their team colours, one of whom is talking loudly into his ancient Nokia as the train pulls in and he prepares to step down onto the platform. "That young fitness bloke—do you remember him?—what year would that have been? 1987? You don't know him? Oh. What year was that? 198—." I return to the page in front of me and re-read: "ways to let someone looking at them see how the world really appears."

Back home, after dinner, the three of us sit around the television to watch election analyst Antony Green present the results as they come in. Jasper and I are hopeful. Ali is sceptical. I remind them, and myself, that Green probably won't be able to call the election tonight because there have been a record number of postal votes, which won't be counted for weeks. But it's so much worse than even Ali had expected, and Green has called it long before it's time for Jasper to go to bed: a Conservative Coalition victory. Trying to be a comfort, Ali reminds me that both sides of the system are broken. Yes, I say, but one side is more broken than the other. He tells me a joke, borrowed from Žižek, which is intended to illustrate the ineptitude of the centre-left. It really doesn't help. I go to bed early, too tired and dispirited to continue reading *Spring*.

Next day, the press is comparing this election to Brexit and the Trump presidency. Back at the shop, people are in need of comfort. Almost without exception, customers who have come in for books talk instead about their disappointment, their despair, how foolish they were to have allowed themselves to hope, the uncomfortable realisation that a vast proportion of the country thinks differently to them, hopes for different things. There is end-times talk. Talk of the end of the Great Barrier Reef, of the Murray-Darling Basin, of swathes of already barely-arable farming land. There is talk of floods and of unseasonal heat, of unseasonal cold and of weather "events." There is even, at one point, talk of secession.

Amid these discussions I find myself returning again and again to Smith's seasonal quartet. I tell customers that I'm reading *Spring* and that, although I didn't plan it thus, it seems the perfect book for both Election Day and election disappointment. I say that Smith is able to hold a mirror up to this moment in this world and that because she is smart and funny and so precise, because she situates this moment and this world in a longer history, because she renders this moment and this world and this wider view personal—via Richard and Paddy and Brittany and Florence and a thousand, thousand other people, via Art and Lux and Sophia and Iris, via Daniel and Elisabeth—and because she insists, despite this, upon the maintenance of a distance between a personal view and the wider, roving perspective of art, because of all these things she is able to be honest about the world—to show it as it really appears—without losing hope. Over the course of the day, many people leave the shop with a copy of *Autumn* (I suggest they start reading the quartet at the beginning, being funny that way). But I feel especially hopeful for the future when one man leaves with *Autumn* as well as both Valeria Luiselli's *Lost Children Archive* and *Tell Me How It Ends*, and both Deborah Levy's *Things I Don't Want to Know* and *The Cost of Living*. When I ask the man which book he'll read first, he says he'll pick at random. I watch him leave with his carry-bag full. I think of the effect those words will have, at this moment, in this world, on the page and beyond.

Of course, many things only begin to make sense later, when I start to write them down. Things like the importance of that distance Smith creates—and keeps—between the personal and the wider, political view of art. Thinking about it now in the moment of writing, that distance is, perhaps, best compared with the space created by Tacita Dean in *Floh*, and described in *Spring* by Richard, which emerges between an unknown photographer, via a flea-market, through the re-presentation of that found picture in the context of contemporary art, and in the light cast by a viewer's consequent "aesthetic attention." What shifts in this space is not the image itself, but our relationship to it. What shifts is the way we look, the way we see. The world can only be revealed as it really is in these photographs because they are no longer personal snapshots. A viewer can only afford them aesthetic attention and see the images whole when not looking for signs of themselves or their loved ones, when not assessing the cut of a dress or lamenting the squint of an eye. And it's this thought that makes me think maybe I'm wrong. Maybe Smith doesn't hold up a mirror to the world as we see it. Maybe what she's doing is repositioning us in relation to that image, redirecting our gaze *away* from the mirror—away from the selfie #nofilter, from Twitter and Snapchat, from the Instagram feed and the Facebook album—*towards* the world as it actually is, now.

X

I'D FORGOTTEN THE FIZZING INSOMNIA that accompanies reading the work of Olivia Laing: the long nights of accelerated thought, something akin to over-caffeination or blue light exposure, but distinguished by a more deeply buried fidget. It's the kind of agitation that leaves ripple marks in sedimentary rock, the insinuation of weather from another time and place. I'd forgotten the sensation of having struck out from the safety of shore: cast adrift from the rhythms of wakefulness and rest, the habits of mind, the structures of language that locate you, me, and every other within it. I'd forgotten the seams of uncertainty that disrupt the self and any attempt to describe it. But, it's mid-2018, I'm reading *Crudo*, and it's all coming back to me now.

I first came across Laing's work when her début, *To the River*, was published in 2011. At that time I was living in a village in Warwickshire, spending the mornings writing at a makeshift desk, drafting a novella in which I reimagined the attempted suicide of a woman and the accidental death of the man who jumped into the Thames from Hammersmith Bridge to save her. In the afternoons, my mind still slick with thoughts of drowning, I walked the Avon canal, sometimes towards Stratford but more often in the opposite direction, past the stables and over the Edstone Aqueduct until I began to tire and turned towards home. When I needed a change of scene, I took the train to London and the British Library where I called up Virginia Woolf's letters and notebooks, scanning drafts of what would become *Mrs Dalloway*. So, when I stumbled upon *To the River* and read on its jacket Woolf, walking, the River Ouse from source to sea, I thought, yes please, and added it to the pile of books I kept handy to the sofa and dipped into in the evenings.

But I didn't read it then. When it was time to leave the village, I packed *To the River* along with the other books I had collected during my stay, paid the excess baggage fees, and returned to my flat in Melbourne, where I found a home for it on bookshelves that were thick with dust after my time away.

In 2013, when Laing published her second book, *The Trip to Echo Spring*, I picked it up from the bookshop where I was now working, took it straight from the United Book Distributors box it arrived in, and carried it home at the end of a late shift. *En route*, stopping for afters at the bar across the street, I read the epigraph from John Berryman's 'Dream Song 36': "Easy, easy, Mr. Bones. I is on your side." Flicking through the pages, I skimmed the seven indications of alcohol dependence as defined by the *Diagnostic and Statistical Manual of Mental Disorders* (or *DSM-IV-TR*), and paused each time I came to a photograph. I lingered over Hemingway with his father; and Fitzgerald standing among a clutter of books and household objects, Zelda kneeling, smiling up at him, two children keeping their distance from the domestic nightmare, but facing the camera, holding it to account; and Tennessee Williams in profile, utterly and unexpectedly beautiful; and Carver, a fish in one hand, a rod in the other; and, most of all, Cheever, caught in motion on his bicycle, something intoxicating about his beaming face, the privacy of the moment of being in a moving body in a swiftly moving world. But after I had drained my glass I put the book in my bag and on the train home I looked out the window, watching for the river crossing when I might otherwise have read. The next morning, before returning to the shop, I placed

The Trip to Echo Spring on the shelf alongside *To the River*. And there they stayed.

Until 2016, that is, when a sales rep gave me an advance copy of *The Lonely City*. It is difficult to say for certain now why it was, finally, that I opened this book and began to read. I have always been captivated by cities and their particular ways of being. At that time, I was teaching an undergraduate course about literature and the city, introducing first year students to the figure of the urban walker, encouraging them to take the temperature of places they more often moved through without thought. Then again, years before, in what has come to feel like someone else's life, I had worked as a curator of contemporary art and found myself increasingly drawn to a number of the artists with whom Laing is also fascinated, in particular Nan Goldin, whose *Heartbeat* (2000-2001) I went to see almost daily at the Centre Pompidou in 2006, when I fled to Paris alone to get my thirtieth birthday out of the way and in private. (Incidentally, the same Centre Pompidou show included Andy Warhol's *Ten Lizes*, which I worked to avoid on my way to Goldin's room. Warhol, I thought: yawn. Laing has since changed my mind about his work, among other things, but more of that later.)

This experience of Goldin's *Heartbeat*—which I would come to associate with Laing's prose, and which is as much a testament to the trust and intimacy that can blossom between a work of art and its viewer as it is of the bond between Goldin and her family of friends—confirmed in me a growing frustration with works that shut down this space for intimate connection. It also led me to curate an exhibition, *Intimacy* (2008), at the Australian Centre for Contemporary Art, and then, almost immediately, to depart from the professional art world. In 2016, although I was no longer working directly with visual art and artists, the potential for art to create a space for either intimacy or alienation—whatever the medium—continued to preoccupy me. Perhaps it was this that drew me to *The Lonely City*. Or, as Laing herself might say, perhaps not.

Whatever the cause, the effect was ecstatic. At the end of another night shift I hustled latecomers out the door, shut up shop, crossed the street and took up my window seat with a glass of wine. I began to read:

> Cities can be lonely places, and in admitting this we see that loneliness doesn't necessarily require physical solitude, but rather an absence or paucity of connection, closeness, kinship: an inability, for one reason or another, to find as much intimacy as is desired.

I read of Laing's move, for love, from England to New York, and when love failed to keep its promises, of her experience of being cast adrift, clinging to the city as a shipwreck survivor might cling to the body of a raft. I read of her other love, for images, and her growing attachment to "the people behind them"— Andy Warhol, Edward Hopper, Valerie Solanas, David Wojnarowicz, Henry Darger, Klaus Nomi, Nan Goldin, Greta Garbo, Jean-Michel Basquiat, and others—"people who had grappled in their lives as well as work with loneliness and its attendant issues." On the train home, blind to the river crossing, I continued to read. And in my flat, I read on into the night and early morning.

XI

WHEN I WOKE, after that night immersed in Laing's lonely city, it was to the image of Garbo, who spent her long retirement walking the streets of New York—"striding around the city in men's shoes and a man's trench coat, taking no shit from anyone, out solely for herself"—and to the bitter aftertaste of Ted Leyson, the paparazzo who stalked her for the last eleven years of her life. Something worried me about the dynamic between Garbo and Leyson—one of those sedimentary ripples I have come to associate with Laing's prose—and it wasn't Leyson's "dehumanising... meat-making" male gaze. Or at least, it wasn't only that. Leyson believed that his stalking of Garbo was an act of love and admiration. From his perverse point of view, his gaze—mediated by the camera lens, one of the technologies Andy Warhol cherished as a means of encountering while keeping his distance from others—was an intimate one. But what of Garbo, who rejected that intimacy and who was, potentially, alienated by it?

Laing's analysis of Garbo and Leyson, which is part of a larger consideration of what it means to be a woman walking alone and unable to escape the male gaze, is riveting. She writes of Garbo's refusal of the constrictions of femininity and her "radical self-possession," even as this refusal, this self-possession, this denial of the intrusive gaze is captured in photographs taken by Leyson as he lurked outside her apartment building and stalked her through the city streets. Among these photographs is the final one taken before she died, which Leyson shot

> through the window of the car that was taking [Garbo] to hospital, her long silver hair down around her shoulders, one veined hand covering the lower portion of her face. She's looking at him through tinted glasses, her expression a queasy combination of fear, scorn and resignation; a gaze that should by rights have cracked the lens.

To look at a person in a private moment of being: this is, surely, part of the appeal of art. It is also part of the appeal of auto/biography, the genre in which all of Laing's work, including her novel, *Crudo*, can be situated. This way of looking was one of the things that drew me back to the Centre Pompidou day after day to sit with Goldin's *Heartbeat*: to bear witness to the intimate lives of others. Goldin's photographs couldn't be more different from Leyson's. *Heartbeat* and the *Ballad of Sexual Dependency* are devoid of the grubby voyeurism that taints Leyson's pictures and the viewer can therefore look without feeling that their gaze is intrusive. Laing's work has the same quality. Her passionate reading of the lives and works of, say, Woolf, Berryman, Darger, and others, but also, importantly, her refusal to moralise about them, means that she is able to capture aspects of her subjects' private lives without shattering the privacy that maintains their sense of self. It was this, among other things, which kept me transfixed as I finished *The Lonely City* and took down from its shelf first *To the River*, then *The Trip to Echo Spring*.

It is my habit, once hooked, to return to the beginning and read an author's work chronologically. My mother tells me it's the historian in me, and I'd be happy to concede the point, but I'm beginning to wonder if this impulse has more in common with a biographical approach than it does a strictly historical reading. And I'm disturbed by it, because I've always been suspicious of overly biographical readings of art. I've taken a curious comfort from the thought that the work and the artist who creates it are not one, that something happens between the mind and the hand which transforms the original thought or image or idea, and that whatever else this transformative process does, it complicates any easy alliance between art and artist at the same time as—hopefully—it strengthens the intimate connection between art and audience.

And yet, back in 2011, reading Woolf's notebooks and letters alongside her published works (chronologically, of course), I was also noting her preoccupation with bodies of water and watching for clues of what I knew was to come. And on that morning after reading *The Lonely City* when I awoke to the image of Garbo looking back and shattering the lens, after I'd made coffee and taken *To the River* down from its shelf, I think I knew that in returning to the beginning (as I then thought) I was also looking for pieces of the puzzle from which a self is composed. The interior world and its armoured exterior, the psychic and the physical geographies of love and loss, intimacy and alienation: these were the coordinates by which I was learning to find my way through Laing's prose. Laing has a gift for stitching her own story to the biographies of the artists and writers to whom she is drawn. And it was a shock when, like Garbo, I found her looking back and shattering the lens of my retrospective reading.

Associated with Laing's practice of auto/biography is a keen awareness of the limitations of the genre—limitations that are symptomatic of the fundamental difficulty of human communication, of being an individual and a citizen, being one member of a community. Reading *The Lonely City*, I noted again and again references to "the essential unknowability of others," "the precarious, imperfect means by which we express our interiors," and "the silences [as described by David Wojnarowicz] of the inner life." In *To the River*, I read—with an "outsider's greedy eye"—details of Virginia Woolf's private and public lives and the personal events that led to Laing's walk along the River Ouse, conscious all the while of "how alone man is, though he can touch and talk and gaze on others of his kind," because "no one but he will ever see [the picture theatre within his head] played, and there is no medium on earth that can accurately catch its luminosity or speed." In *The Trip to Echo Spring*, I read of the intimate connection between a writer's life and work, and of the problem of "the common or garden issue of literary biography: that while a writer may draw very deeply on events they've experienced or felt, what they make of them is never straightforwardly factual and cannot be treated as such."

"It's not always possible to plot where something starts," Laing writes in *To the River* of her search for the source of the Ouse. And yet, in auto/biography we seek to excavate the beginning of a narrative, to find the source and from it, with hindsight, to elaborate a pattern of cause and effect. Laing goes back to the beginning—of, say, Darger's difficult childhood—she discovers patterns—in, say, the suicides of Hemingway's and Berryman's fathers and their subsequent alcoholism—but, importantly, she writes against the unnatural way in which hindsight can flatten a life as it was lived. Here she is on Woolf, and the temptation to read her work in light of her later suicide:

> Some patterns can only be observed at great distance, it's true, but in order to view life in this way something else must be sacrificed, for when we look with hindsight from the final outcome back, we see events inflected with a meaning that the one who lived them never grasped. I don't believe there is a single person who's not troubled sometimes in the course of their days by a sense of occlusion or tenuousness, a sense that their actions occur within such a great expanse of darkness on either side that they might prove at the last incoherent and devoid of sense.

Thus, for all that Laing shines a light on the events lived by her subjects, she remains at a remove from the theatre of their inner lives at the time of living. Even as she reads their archives and published works, as she looks into their lives of art—in "some devoted act of seeing"—she is (necessarily) still an outsider looking in, doing her job as "scrutiniser and witness."

XII

In *Crudo*, Laing's first novel, the ground has shifted again. She is still an outsider: this is, for Laing, the natural position for an artist. But her point of view—an autofictional eye, principally narrated in the third person, borrowing from the life and work of Kathy Acker—is directed towards the inner life and the picture theatre of the mind. As it must be for a citizen, this theatre is concerned with the world stage, in particular the events of the northern summer of 2017: wildfires across Europe, the conflagration at Grenfell Tower, threats to the NHS, the calving of the Larsen-C ice shelf, the rollback of Obamacare, the sacking of James Comey, the flight of young men from Mosul, a woman who liveblogs her rape on Instagram, North Korea's threat to bomb Guam, far-right rallies in Charlottesville, the resignation of Steve Bannon, the removal of Confederate statues across the United States, Sinéad O'Connor's breakdown on YouTube, floods in Houston, North Korea's detonation of a sixth nuclear bomb, further threats to the NHS, the development of facial recognition software, further threat of nuclear war. "Kathy hated it, living at the end of the world," writes Laing, "but she couldn't help but find it interesting, watching people herself included compulsively foul their nest." Yet despite her anxiety that "she might exhaust the present and find herself out at the front, alone on the crest of time," she reasons that "[s]ince there'd be no end to it she might as well consign it to paper." Kathy records everything in her notebook, she trawls the internet, in particular her "scrying glass, Twitter," and captures in the "nearly right now" of the summer of 2017 the inner life at the end of the world, living in the glare of global events, of Donald Trump and Kim Jong-un, in "the permanent present of the id."

Alongside the public events of May to September 2017 is a private occasion. *Crudo* begins: "Kathy, by which I mean I, was getting married." And the novel's countdown to the end of the world is also a countdown to marriage, a portrait of the radical shift from a life lived solo to one that is shared. This is not an easy adjustment to make. It has unlooked-for effects upon the inner self and its relation to the outside world. "You think you know yourself inside out when you live alone," observes Kathy, "but you don't, you believe you are a calm untroubled or at worst melancholic person, you do not realise how irritable you are, how any little thing, the wrong kind of touch or tone, a lack of speed in answering a question, a particular cast of expression will send you into apoplexy because you are unchill, because you have not learnt how to soften your borders, how to make room." But how do you learn to make room, as a private individual and a citizen, how do you soften your intimate borders at a time when young men trying to escape Mosul are tortured by Iraqi security forces who suspect them of being IS combatants, when "fire and fury" are brewing between the United States and North Korea, when the UK is fortifying its borders against Europe, when everywhere borders are being strengthened against refugees for whom no government, it seems, will soften and make room?

Kathy rails against the policing of geopolitical, personal, and aesthetic borders. Just as "she barely regard[s] herself as female," she barely regards her fiction as novelistic. The form of the novel is a "hopeless apparatus of guesswork and supposition, with which Kathy liked to have as little traffic as possible. She wrote fiction, sure, but she populated it with the already extant, the pre-packaged and readymade." Adopting a method reminiscent of her description of Woolf's work, Laing (which is also to say Kathy) experiments with memoir and biography and has composed a fiction that "contain[s] elements of each": "Writing, she can be anyone. On the page the I dissolves, becomes amorphous, proliferates wildly." In *Crudo*, gender and genre are equally unstable: "Transitioning, [Kathy] loved the word, with its sense of constant emergence and zero arrival."

Transitioning—that state of perpetual emergence, which refuses the falsely fortified borders between here and there, mine and yours, male and female, fact and fiction—might also offer a mode of obfuscating the forward thrust of time. (Or perhaps not. Kathy is getting older. Cruelly, transitioning doesn't appear to accommodate the constant emergence of youth, the zero arrival at middle age.) It is this that gives *Crudo* the impression of the permanent present (even as it is principally narrated in the past tense), that rare quality of capturing the experience of living personally and politically in the "nearly right now."

Kathy meditates upon the problem of historical representation in a way that recalls Laing's consideration of hindsight in earlier works. Looking back at New York in the 1980s, at the "epicentre of the epicentre" of the AIDS crisis, which is, also, the epicentre of *The Lonely City*, Kathy observes:

> This was the problem with history, it was too easy to provide furnishings but forget the attitudes, the way you became a different person according to what knowledge was available, what experiences were fresh and what had not yet arisen in a personal or global frame. ... She was trying to reconstruct attitudes, to understand ambient levels of prejudice and fear.

Crudo is, among other things, a rollcall of the attitudes, prejudices, and fears that coloured the northern summer of 2017. With that luminosity and speed which, in *To the River*, Laing found wanting in any attempt to communicate the picture theatre of the mind,

Crudo captures the relentless newsreel of the global frame and the experience of living within it: the shifts in Kathy's person in light of fresh knowledge and the context of current events.

To read *Crudo* is to live inside the skin of one of the archives Laing reads so passionately in *To the River*, *The Trip to Echo Spring*, and *The Lonely City*. A novel that captures without containing a single summer, it is already out of date and unlikely ever to become dated. Archives show their age in curious ways; they are at once as old as the time they document and render that time perpetually now. As such *Crudo* embodies, *par excellence*, constant emergence and zero arrival. Kathy may struggle to soften her borders but, in her first work of fiction, Laing has found a way to make room for the intimate connection that can exist between art and its audience so that a reader may look, without shattering the lens, onto the picture theatre of an inner life.

XIII

NOW IT'S MARCH 1987 and Beverley Farmer is composing a short story that will become 'Vase with Red Fishes.' It begins—not the story, but her composition—with a Matisse print, *Intérieur, bocal aux poisons rouges*: "On a stand with long grey wooden legs is a jar of thick glass more than half full of water in which are circling two goldfish, *poisons rouge*, red-gold fishes nosing at the fragmenting shrunken and swollen shadows they inhabit." Later that same month, Farmer buys two nannygais from the Prahran Market. "Nannygais (redfish!)." She stuffs their bellies with herbs picked fresh from the garden and bakes them. She tests the texture of their flesh, watches their colour ripen, sees it shift from silver to white, white to red, red wounded to blue:

> They are not red-*skinned*—they have silvery white skin tightly covered in a mesh, a red net with a sheen, denser at the peak of the back and more open and pale lower down. A rack of dorsal spines, fins clear red, finely braided. Blood has tarnished their eyes. The pupils are hollow—you can see into the dim caves in their skulls.
>
> At the base of the great wound behind the head and in the skin along the slit at the edge of the belly—a bluish pearly gleam.

Farmer is a sensualist. She touches the world with words. Reading her at her best is something like watching a sculptor at work.

I read *A Body of Water* and think about baking red fish stuffed with herbs picked fresh from the garden. But I'm rubbish with whole fish, discomforted by the very mesh and dorsal spines and fin, by the cavity of the skull, by the blood-tarnished eyes, and especially by the wound that, on the page, give back to Farmer's nannygais their three-dimensional existence. Instead, I plant a Virginia creeper against the shed wall where I can see it through the study window. "The Virginia creeper is turning papery yellow and glossy red," writes Farmer (and as I write this, it is), "translucent leaves press against the window panes, dark-veined, cobwebbed. Ivy and pigeons: they creep into the smallest space and are hard to dislodge; they've crept into a story while I've been working on it, huddled over the radiator munching apples."

Ali and I are renting and I don't know how many autumns I'll have to watch the Virginia creeper creep into the crevices of the shed wall, to see it fill the spaces behind the camellia and the daphne and the self-seeded pumpkin. But I plant it anyway. Planting the creeper, watching its forked tendrils catch hold of the creviced wall, its leaves turn yellow, red, russet before they fall, watching new leaves bud and begin at last to unfurl, new tendrils shoot and catch and creep, all this and more is another way of reading Farmer, another way of learning from her to read the world.

XIV

In *The World Was Whole*, the beautifully curated follow-up to her award-winning *Small Acts of Disappearance*, the Australian essayist and poet Fiona Wright considers how to make a home in a precarious world. This is a world with which we are all too familiar, one marked by "unspecified global threat, imminent ecological disaster, increasing workplace uncertainty." It is a world of serial displacements, in which people are "unhomed" by the machinations of global capital, by environmental catastrophe, by the "everyday injuries" of casualised employment and insecure rental housing. But for Wright, it is also a world made chaotic by chronic illness, specifically a combination of physical rumination—unwilled vomiting—with severe and enduring anorexia nervosa. *The World Was Whole* is at once more personal and more political than *Small Acts of Disappearance*, which focused primarily on Wright's illness, her experience of being in an unsettled (and unsettling) body. In this second collection, Wright draws on that experience to illuminate other forms of precarity and to investigate new ways of narrating them.

During her first year of university, when she was nineteen, Wright was unhomed by illness. It rendered her body "unsafe... uncertain... a thing I did not know." The nature of rumination, according to which Wright's body rejects certain foods, demanded that she learn to pay close attention to "the small details of what I was eating and how my body was reacting." As she reflects in the essay 'To Run Away from Home,' "I think I very soon found reassurance, found some security in those minutiae." Wright's attention to reassuringly small details became a fixation as her restrictive eating developed into anorexia. But it is also via these small details, the matter which makes up the everyday and is too often dismissed as mundane, that Wright has come to explore what it means to inhabit a body, to be at home, in the world.

The ideas Wright introduces in 'To Run Away from Home' are developed throughout *The World Was Whole*. In the book's first essay, she draws upon Bachelard, in particular his discussion in *The Poetics of Space* of "the 'passionate liaison' of our bodies and the spaces we inhabit, our homes." I see Bachelard everywhere: in W.G. Sebald and Esther Kinsky, in Jorge Consiglio, in Beverley Farmer, in Virginia Woolf. He is, for me, intimately associated with the thought of home, with ways of being on the page, in the world, and across every dimension between them. So it's a relief to read Wright credit Bachelard directly, to be able to read her essays in the light of his phenomenology without worrying (overly) that I'm imposing my own eccentric view of the world and our place within it, without, in some sense, "unhoming" her words as I read them.

The intimate connections between the body and the spaces we come to think of as home—among them the "habits of movement" that at once shape those spaces and are shaped by them—are invoked again and again in these essays. They are there on a return to the family home, beneath bare feet, in the sensation of carpet "thick and creamy as Greek yoghurt." They are there, after every move, at every new house, in Wright's placement of her desk beneath a window, "so I can watch the people walking past, the light shifting, across the day." They are there in the maintenance of daily rituals—rising early, writing at cafés—in Newtown, Sydney, as much as in Reykjavík or Shanghai. And they are there for Wright, too, upon the return from hospital—a place that imposes on the body its own routines—in unpacking her bag, vacuuming her bedroom, and watering her garden; in coming home to "the habits I have that shape it and are shaped by it, the small delights it gives me across the day." Back home, Wright walks through her neighbourhood "just to feel it on [her] skin." It is, for her as for Bachelard, everyday, joyful, and deeply sensual connections such as these that make a home and shelter the thinking, dreaming self who lives there.

But, as the essays in *The World Was Whole* demonstrate so vividly, the passionate liaison between body and space is fragile and, increasingly, the connections between the body and the home are unsettled. Even before she was unhomed by illness, Wright's connection to the place of her birth was complicated: "I didn't feel I fit there. ... But what I came to realise, slowly, was that the place didn't fit me." This awkward fit is partly to do with the idea of suburbia and the "almost eugenic" association of these spaces with physical health. But it is also a side-effect of European invasion and the violent dispossession of Indigenous Australians. The world Wright describes in this collection is built on stolen land. Her complication of the idea of home is indebted to a kind of ur-unhoming that has severed the connection between settlers and their "old home"—"I don't have an ancestral home," she writes, "I don't think any white Australian does"—and, with the perpetual return of repressed colonial violence, renders their position forever uncanny.

The legacy of invasion is only one of the forms of unsettlement explored in *The World Was Whole*. Elsewhere, Wright reflects upon the effects of gentrification on formerly familiar places. She captures the alienating consequences of the property market in a city like Sydney where "the median house price is now more than twelve times the median income of its inhabitants," and she exposes the politics of rental housing in Australia where almost half of renters live under what is officially termed "financial housing stress." 'Little Heart,' an essay about being in Shanghai on a writer's residency, is also about the importance of "rootedness" as "another way of knowing one's place in the world." In China, Wright learns of the government's plans to "relocate ten million people over the next two years, for massive infrastructure projects," and describes the country's "floating population" of around 245 million low-skilled workers, who are principally engaged in the manufacture of "Disney toys, and iPhones," and live in dormitories "far from their *hùkou*, their official household registry, which gives them access to government services like healthcare, housing and schooling." Again, in 'A Regular Choreography,' on a tour of Iceland, driving "through vast and empty flood plains, dusty grey and littered with gibber-like stones," she repeatedly hears that "there used to be a town here, there used to be a fishing village here; once, my family used to farm sheep here, but it moved, we moved, after the volcano."

In the face of such radical and far-reaching unsettlement, can we continue to speak of home? Is it enough to return to habits of movement and seek shelter there? The answer, it seems, is yes, and also no. Part of the appeal of Bachelard's poetics of space, with its celebration of the bodily rhythms and daily rituals of home-making, is that we can carry "home" with us wherever we go. Thus, in Iceland and China, Wright can return to the habits of movement that keep her grounded in Sydney in an attempt to heal what she describes as the "wounds" of travel:

> What I like about [Bachelard's] formulation is that it's hopeful, it suggests that even with great distance from or discomfort with any idea of home, the memory of wholeness, of homeliness is always alive somewhere within us, always animating our bodies, even and especially when we're not aware of it at all.

But not all wounds can be healed. One of the threads that stitch together the essays in this collection is the desire to understand what happens when the body—that home that is thought to give us shelter—cannot be made comfortable in any straightforward sense, or according to dominant narratives of illness and recovery. According to Wright, the idea of wholeness and of being at home

> is more complicated for those of us whose bodies are unsimple, for those of us who have been ill, especially chronically so—for those of us who go hungry. We're overwritten with different stories, some that contradict, some that complement, and some that simply cannot comprehend the diagrams we carry of that first home, and this process never stops. For those of us who write, for whom inscription is something we do with our bodies, rather than something that is simply done to them, the formulation can never be this clear. I don't want to go home. And yet I do. I can't go home, and yet I never left.

For a writer, inscription is another of those habits of movement that give shelter, even in a storm, and Wright seeks to understand her illness as much via writing as via medical treatment. What is clear, however, is that new forms of inscription are required by those whose bodies are unsimple, who feel unhomed and yet retain the memory of wholeness, for those whose person and place in the world have been overwritten and whose stories are repeatedly marginalised by narratives that insist upon a single (simple) trajectory from illness to health, grief to joy, precarity to security and so on.

Towards the end of 'To Run Away From Home,' describing her own experience, and that of many of her friends, Wright states that "our new normal is a less settled one, less homed, but I don't think we have, yet, the new narratives and metaphors we need to understand this." We live in time as well as in space and the stories we tell ourselves—the ways we make sense of our place in the world—are time-based. They don't always tell time in the same way, according to the same rhythms, the same measures of experience, but they tell time, nevertheless. The essays in this collection—each of which strives towards a new narrative of unsettlement—are as much concerned with time as they are with space. Drawing on the work of Iris Marion Young, Wright is engaged in an extended meditation upon the differences between the transcendent and the immanent, those "two kinds of time in which we live all of our lives":

> Transcendent time is that rare, luminous time of important or startling events—like travel, or those intense first weeks of falling in love, or the sweeping grief of sudden loss, the shock of an argument that wounds. These are moments where we are transported out of our regular selves and assumptions, where time feels different, slowed, or furiously hastened; it is time that breaks the rules of everyday life. Immanent time, however, *is* the rules—it is regular, unruffled, it passes mostly without us noticing. But we need immanent time, to rest, to reflect, to maintain our sense of self; and it is within immanent time that we live more completely and more often, less intensely. It is here we are at home, wherever we may physically be.

Just as we do from those Bachelardian habits of movement, from the routines of immanent time we construct a home that travels with us wherever we go. These everyday habits and routines—these rules, if you like—at once induce a kind of forgetfulness—when I walk to my desk, when I sit down and take up my pen, I do it thoughtlessly—and they provide the conditions necessary to reflect upon that thoughtlessness, among other things.

But, in the face of workplace, ecological, economic, and physical precarity, immanent time—as well as the home for rest and reflection, for thought that it affords—is under threat. In their attention to the events of immanent time, to the small rituals that make a home, and the everyday injuries that unsettle it, the essays in *The World Was Whole* nourish novel forms of inscription. Here, in prose that at times recalls the traditional personal essay, at others is more fragmentary, and always builds according to a logic of association, Wright has composed a grammar of home that makes sense of the "new normal" of unsettlement, and looks forward to ways of being—joyfully, in body and in mind, even, hopefully, at home—in a precarious world.

XV

It's 2018 and I'm preparing a pair of lectures on Beverley Farmer's novella *Alone*, published in 1980. I've taught the book for three years now, but this will be the last time. Two years ago, students commented that they found the narrative strange and dark and that they were glad they'd read it. Last year, one student suggested that it be taught only after these same strange and dark sections had been "crossed out." Now, I've been called to a meeting at which the subject coordinator announces that in the future it will no longer be appropriate to teach texts that address thoughts of suicide, matter-of-fact descriptions of rape. I don't say: Isn't it curious that at the height of the #MeToo movement we're silencing discussion of gendered violence in the classroom? I don't ask: Will *Hamlet* and *Tess of the D'Urbervilles* also be removed from the curriculum? (Only later do I remember that Hardy hasn't been taught for years, his characters deemed insufficiently "relatable.") After the meeting, I realise that my tongue is sore, blistered from where I've been biting it.

There are other, equally disturbing reasons for the disjuncture in 2018 between *Alone* and the world beyond the page. Part of the appeal of teaching this book has always been how recognisable its depiction of the city in 1959 still is in the twenty-first century. I show students archival photographs of Melbourne, then and now. I give them an exercise, tell them to pick a key location of *Alone*—the Carlton United Brewery, Swanston Street, the Docks—and read it as a palimpsest. We talk of Shirley Iris Nunn (S.I.N.), the book's narrator, and her overlayering of the literature of the city, of Baudelaire, Eliot, Joyce, Woolf: "[t]here are no new starts, no new leaves," Shirley writes. "Palimpsests. I am a palimpsest." We talk about the overlayering of place. I encourage students to discover the still-visible, still-liveable layers of history in the city. But every year, less and less of this city is left to live. Actual palimpsests are levelled, replaced with another ugly, schmick and largely empty high-rise with an "historical" panel tucked into some remote corner of its foyer: the city turned museum piece, so that its story might be properly erased.

Around the same time, I visit the Australian Centre for the Moving Image to see a screening of Stanley Crammer's 1959 adaptation of Nevil Shute's novel, *On the Beach*. It's brilliant. I love every moment of it. Even the way it seems so horribly prescient in the light of Trump's red button and North Korea's nuclear tests. But later, I'm horrified to recall how much more at home I felt in the post-nuclear, post-apocalyptic Melbourne of Crammer's film, how much more (forgive me) "relatable" was the screen city than the pockmarked demolition site I walk into, after the credits roll.

Outside, there's a man standing in front of St. Paul's Cathedral preaching sin, hell, and damnation. He's wearing a royal blue bomber jacket with a sateen finish. Across its back, a slogan: REPENT OR PERISH. The PERISH is written in a font set aflame in orange and red. Later, on the tram, after the river crossing when we're out of the city proper, I open my book—J.L. Carr's *A Month in the Country*—and read: "So, each day, I released a few more inches of a seething cascade of bones, joints and worm-riddled vitals frothing over the fiery weir."

But it will get worse, much worse, even before the Federal Election, before the loss of hope, before the real end-times talk begins. It's April 2019 and the body of a woman, Natalina Angok, has been discovered in Celestial Avenue, one of the blind alleyways leading off Little Bourke Street. She's been raped and murdered. It was also in Celestial Avenue that Catherine, Shirley Iris Nunn's friend and lover, was raped in *Alone*. Now are the worlds on and beyond the page in horrendous alignment. No new starts. No new leaves. Palimpsests.

XVI

"REMINISCENCES OF SELF are reminiscences of place," writes Susan Sontag in her essay on Walter Benjamin, 'Under the Sign of Saturn.' "The work of memory," she goes on, "collapses time." It makes a ruin of chronology, creates the space for a topographical and forever fragmented reading of what has passed.

Buenos Aires, Madrid, Málaga, La Mancha, Almagro, Barcelona, Heilbronn, Heidelberg, Berlin, Athens, Los Golondrinas. In *All My Goodbyes*, a novella by Mariana Dimópulos (who has herself written a critical study of Benjamin's work), each of these sites of memory is cut loose from chronology, becoming a piece of a puzzle from which reader and narrator attempt to decipher the history here described.

For Sontag, via Benjamin, "a book is not only a fragment of the world but itself a little world... [and] the best way to understand [it] is also to enter [its] space." To enter the space of *All My Goodbyes* is to cross a threshold into a broken world. "I had as many pieces as a broken vase," says the book's unnamed narrator, "and I never found a way to put them back together or even to number my porcelain remains." Like forensic archaeologists, we sift through the debris left behind by the narrator's restless European years: the people and the places; the serial, menial jobs; the budding relationships; the houses that could have been made a home. All abandoned. "These are all my crimes: all my goodbyes."

XVII

A YOUNG WOMAN leaves her home and family in Buenos Aires and spends the next decade travelling across Europe. "Why, or to what end? Sometimes I don't know." The daughter of a physicist—"a well-intentioned butcher of innocence"—she is instructed by him in the habit of scepticism: "The blue of the sky? Just an effect of the Earth's atmospheric gases and the light of the sun"; "Precambrian stones are fundamentally no different to the wings of a fly. ... [Stone] simply holds its form for a longer period of time"; "Rest is a form of movement"; "[S]trictly speaking, nowhere existed anywhere."

All My Goodbyes is, in part, an interrogation of the relationship between time and space. As such it captures the paradox inherent in the physical world as we currently understand it. Carlo Rovelli describes this in his *Seven Brief Lessons on Physics*:

> A university student attending lectures on general relativity in the morning and others on quantum mechanics in the afternoon might be forgiven for concluding that his professors are fools. ... In the morning the world is curved space where everything is continuous; in the afternoon it is a flat space where quanta of energy leap.
>
> The paradox is that both theories work remarkably well.

The structure of *All My Goodbyes* echoes that of quantum mechanics, in which the flow of time and the curvature of space give way to quanta, or "grains of space and matter [that] no longer contain the variable 'time'." According to Rovelli, these "materialize in a place... [only] when colliding headlong with something else." Hence the narrator's father's insistence that, "strictly speaking," nowhere exists and that rest is a form of movement. Reality—space and time—takes shape in movement, via interaction.

By this reading, the fragmented nature of *All My Goodbyes* is not simply that of a postmodern non-linear narrative. There is nothing simple about this novella. Its narrative is not fragmented only because the work of memory makes a ruin of the forward flow of time. Yes, the narrator is remembering what she describes as her "pilgrim years." Yes, she is working to piece together her "porcelain remains." But the brokenness of her narrative is not solely a reflection of the frailty of memory. Reality is broken, in the sense that it is composed of grains of space that, in Rovelli's words, "cannot be ordered in a common succession of 'instants'." This novella captures the unnerving experience of scientific doubt: a contagious sense, which the narrator learned early from her father, that the world is not what it seems. Dimópulos' protagonist has not found a way to restore the instants of her experience, to make her history whole again, because there is no chronology—only leaps from one event to another and suggestive interactions between them. Only arrival and departure.

XVIII

A YOUNG WOMAN leaves her home and family in Buenos Aires and spends the next decade travelling across Europe: "I... regarded myself as incapable of sleeping in a bed, sitting in a chair, inhabiting a room, for too long." Over the course of her pilgrim years, the narrator of *All My Goodbyes* moves restlessly between cities, jobs, relationships. Playing first at being an artist ("what young people do when they're in Madrid and they're Latin American"), and then (briefly) a tourist, she becomes in her restlessness a kind of secular pilgrim, a perpetual foreigner who—according to the logic of global capital with its insatiable demand for cheap migrant labour—works as a shelf-stacker at Ikea, a parts-sorter at a used-car factory, a maid-of-all-work at a hotel, *et cetera*.

In her book *Wanderlust*, Rebecca Solnit argues that pilgrimage is "one of the fundamental structures a journey can take—the search for something, if only one's own transformation." Citing anthropologists Nancy Frey and Victor and Edith Turner, Solnit is particularly interested in the ways in which the experience of pilgrimage affects the pilgrim's perceptions of time, space, and self. According to Frey, pilgrims "develop a changing sense of time." Likewise, for the Turners, as paraphrased by Solnit, pilgrimage is "a state of being between one's past and future identities and thus outside the established order, in a state of possibility."

The liminality of the pilgrim's experience, that state of being between—including, perhaps, mid-leap between one quanta event and another—is similar in important ways to Valeria Luiselli's experience of being permanently "alien," a "non-resident in New York." In 'Other Rooms,' one of the essays in her début collection *Sidewalks*, Luiselli relates conversations with doormen who "are usually emigrants of some kind, metaphorically, if not literally." These men inhabit the threshold of residential buildings across New York, the kind of liminal space and time that pilgrims take to the road in search of. As such, and like the narrator of *All My Goodbyes*, they understand the need to keep moving, the imperative to interpose oneself between strange places. As Luiselli tells it:

> What you have to do, [the doorman] said... is to get out of here as often as you can. That way you get to know yourself better. Only come back to have a bath and eat, never to sleep, because the more often you spend the night in different places—rooms, pensions, hotels, borrowed couches, other people's beds—the better. ... We should all participate in a certain amount of housing polygamy if we want to be true to the millenarian edict: Know thyself.

The possibilities of liminal space—of being at the threshold between arrival and departure—are, it seems, a contributing factor in the desire for perpetual movement. This threshold space cannot be pinned down in time—it hasn't *happened*, as such, but is always in a state of becoming. Hence, Benjamin's celebration of being in movement. Like those other rooms of Luiselli's essay, for Benjamin "space is... teeming with possibilities, positions, intersections, passages, detours." Cross the threshold, decide to stay in place, and time works its dark magic. What was possible instead becomes a constraint.

Reminiscing about the cities in which she resided during her European years, the narrator of *All My Goodbyes* describes the effect of time on her experience of a place:

> The arrival—from dinner, say, or from the supermarket. The setting of the handbag on the floor. The glance around the room.

> What is that chest of drawers, that bed? What is that rug (if there is a rug)? What are those curtains? Suddenly the chair is archaic, there is no use for it. The bedroom is abandoned, the bathroom and its mirrors incomprehensible. How can it be abandoned, I wonder, if until so recently it was my very own room? ... And yet, it has all become unfathomable to me. Did I really think I'd been living within these four walls this whole time? It was just an illusion. A lacklustre magic trick, utterly profane.

Time alienates the narrator from place perhaps because, even when she has come to rest, it continues to move relentlessly forward. And yet her reminiscences, which move against the forward flow of time, collapse chronology and position the narrator in a way her physicist father would have considered impossible.

Throughout the novella, the narrator and the people with whom she interacts attempt to make sense of her perpetual movement. As she tells it:

> If I stay, I stay. If I go, I go. This thought was soothing in the beginning, but then it wasn't anymore. In the beginning I'd just think something logical, and it would calm me down. In the beginning I'd just say 'it's logical', and I'd feel perfectly fine. I moved around logically, from one new city to the next, one new bedroom to the next. And it worked the other way, too: if I stayed, I stayed because it was rational to do so. But soon my reasons grew like a bouquet. In Berlin and Heilbronn, I spent my time contemplating all the rational flowers, morning and night. I call them flowers, but I am suspicious of my own words; if I'd really had a bouquet of reasons, I would have wanted to count them and pull all their petals off. But my reasons had no petals, and no perfume.

What are these reasons with neither petals nor perfume that the narrator seeks to identify and then destroy? Several are suggested throughout the novella: the need to leave home; the desire to avoid the "rodent wheel of real life"; the inability, as Blaise Pascal would have it (in the epigraph with which the book begins), of human beings to "stay quietly in their own chamber"; the narrator's "mean spirit," her avoidance of introspection, her compulsion to move on to the next thing and the next and the next; and the facts of our elemental make-up: "we know from our hydrogen and our oxygen that we are water as well as dust. And water runs."

In Berlin, Julia—a trauma therapist with whom the narrator lives—diagnoses her "suitcase syndrome." In Heidelberg, the narrator marries a man named Alexander and "imagine[s] that he could be reason enough [to stay]." "Those imaginings cost me nothing," she remarks, "[a]nd sometimes I delighted in them secretly, like a stowaway, knowing full well they would never become a reality." Ultimately, and in keeping with the novella's sceptical strain, the quest for finding a reason, for making reliable sense out of the narrator's restlessness, is itself rendered doubtful. "What is 'solved'?" asks Benjamin in his 1928 essay, 'One-Way Street':

> Do not all the questions of our lives, as we live, remain behind us like foliage obstructing our view? To uproot this foliage, even to thin it out, does not occur to us. We stride on, leave it behind, and from a distance it is indeed open to view, but indistinct, shadowy, and all the more enigmatically entangled.

Returned to Buenos Aires, recalling her pilgrim years, the narrator of *All My Goodbyes* would pluck the petals, thin the shadowy foliage of the view of her past, number and restore the pieces of her porcelain remains. But if there was a solution to the question of her perpetual movement, she has left it behind. And because there is no way of re-ordering her history chronologically, the events of her life, as she has lived it, must remain puzzlingly entangled.

XIX

A YOUNG WOMAN leaves her home and family in Buenos Aires and spends the next decade travelling across Europe. She plays at being an artist, then a tourist, but eventually becomes that cornerstone of global capital, a (female) migrant worker from the South in service to the North. Employed as a maid-of-all-work in Berlin, the narrator of *All My Goodbyes* tries "to wipe that sad, servile smile off [her] face... in vain." In Heidelberg, where she is one of many Ikea shelf-stackers (confined, as her Turkish co-worker would have it, by the laws of "modern slavery"), she comes to understand that

> we *were* Ikea shelf-stackers. We behaved like obedient planets each spinning in our own orbit, according to the gravitational laws of our boss. From kitchenware to interior decoration, from the arrangement of plates to sheets, via every imaginable prerequisite for the perfect European home.

Again, at an auto-parts factory—which is, in keeping with the experience of Southern and feminised labour, a forty kilometre bus ride from the city of Heidelberg—a Polish co-worker describes the narrator as "a good slave," to which: "First I'm offended, then I defend myself; much later, I concede defeat."

Throughout *All My Goodbyes*, there are numerous threads to the interrogation of this North-South dynamic. The question of labour is central to the narrative and extends beyond the hemispheric to incorporate economic migrants from the Global South—

Eastern European, Turkish, Southeast Asian, *et cetera*. Of one of her lovers, Stefan (via whom she eventually returns to Buenos Aires), the narrator reports:

> He talked about how they manufactured teacups in Cambodia which sold for a pittance in Australia and Singapore. About the Australians who bought them in the supermarket, and then donate[d] twenty cents to a UNICEF campaign at the register. Didn't I think this was magnificent? Wasn't our world a work of art?

The persistence of colonial conceptions about—and uses of—the South also resonates throughout the book. At a picnic in Heidelberg, the narrator encounters a man "who apparently hadn't been informed of my origins ('aren't you Turkish?') [and] was busy disparaging the politics of Latin America." She goes on:

> He'd travelled to several countries in the Americas and had confirmed for himself the backwardness of our ideas and the corruption of our institutions. ... In the wake of my cultural superior's comments, a very civilised discussion unfolded on the triumphs of liberty and reason, and although a few of them revealed, like an unstitched hem, the guilt behind their Nazi past and the misdeeds of colonialism, to which Europe still owed a great deal of its wealth and progress, the group as a whole seemed terribly satisfied with themselves and with their cordial, democratic world.

According to this logic, Europe continues to stand for freedom, reason, and civilised enlightenment; the South for corruption, emotion, and stunted development. The narrator sees through this. She can see the burden of Europe "weighing heavily" upon Alexander's shoulders, the way that, when he speaks of "European traditionalism," of freedom and social security, he uses words "that [crawl] out of his mouth like tiny insects" and is forced to "rub his lips to prevent them from stinging him." She sees this because she understands the true relation of freedom to slavery: "My freedom always implies the slavery of another. So, my heart asks (and at heart I'm no good): if I enslave myself, does that mean someone else is set free?"

There is, over the course of the narrator's pilgrim years, a curious form of self-enslavement. Unlike many migrant workers from the South, she is not bound by the need to send money home. She is trained as a biologist, has a job in the family business back in Buenos Aires, and, in Germany, is frequently offered the opportunity to find work at a university or in a research laboratory. Is she slumming it? This is one of the novella's questions that remains unsolved. Certainly, the narrator is keen to assure the reader of her "mean spirit" and the narrative is stitched together by her persistent refrain that "at heart, I'm no good." There is in her need for perpetual movement a suggestion of Benjamin's melancholic temperament, that particular "faithlessness" that leads to "eternal voyaging." Likewise, there is a suggestion of the pilgrim's desire "to make their journey harder, recalling the origin of the word travel in *travail*, which means work [and] suffering."

As much as she labours alongside other foreign workers, the narrator remains separate from them. At Ikea, her Turkish and Latvian co-workers subvert their enslavement via escalating acts of sabotage—they break plates, stain sheets, rip the ears from soft toys. "Many mornings," the narrator remembers, "on my way to work, I resolved to join forces with the Turk and the Latvian, to praise their sabotage with my primordial tongue and convince them of my potential worth. I tried and I could not." Thus, the narrator is "a good slave." She enslaves herself and finds a kind of freedom of movement in the uncertainty of migrant labour. Unlike the Turk and the Latvian, and the makers of teacups in Cambodia, the narrator is free to be in perpetual movement, in the leap between this event and the next. In Berlin, at the point of becoming "sealed and approved," she throws her residency card into the river. "[T]hat night," she later recalls, "was the most triumphant of all, because I had nothing in my pockets, not even my own name." Being bad at heart, she chooses to remain undocumented at the threshold of arrival and departure.

XX

AND YET, A WOMAN, no longer young, returns to Buenos Aires after a decade spent travelling across Europe. Her father has died, but she is unable to remain among her brothers and their families and continues to move, this time to Patagonia, to a farm near Los Golandrinas. Here she takes a job as a fruit-picker and falls in love with Marco, a man "happily tied down" to "his life on the mountain."

In 'One-Way Street,' Benjamin suggests that "in a love affair, most people seek an eternal homeland," and it is in love that the narrator of *All My Goodbyes* believes that she has "finally found [her] place": "The planet has stopped spinning. And I've stopped with it." Love counters physics and scientific scepticism. Come to rest, the narrator comes also to believe that

> my father had lied to me. The little house [on the mountain]... was irrefutable proof of this. For the first time in my life I could sit and recline without a shred of scepticism, trusting completely in the resilience of chairs and beds. Anyone could come along with their science now and refute the evidence of my nights and days. ... Because love exists and the place exists.

Reality takes shape in interaction. Not, in this instance, the interaction of perpetual movement, but the interaction of the event of love. In this place, time—the past and the future—also exist. In love, Marco and the narrator "promise each other something akin to the future," and at Los Golondrinas the narrator begins to look back upon all her goodbyes. "I was there," she says, "to swallow the bitter pill of my love for those distant people I'd left for dead, so many years ago."

In love, come to rest at Los Golondrinas, the narrator believes that she has become "whole," that she has a chronological past, present, and future. But the world is granular. It takes shape via the perpetual movement between "all [her] crimes: all [her] goodbyes." And, given that this is a narrative reminiscence, the narrator's world ultimately takes shape in the violent light cast by the brutal crime that is committed at Los Golondrinas:

> After all my travels, all those years lost and won and lost again; after testing a thousand times the raw stock of my being, which never seemed to cook; when at last I had found a man and I had loved him, they called me up so I could see how the story ended: the living room covered in blood from wall to wall, the ransacked house, the abandoned axe.

XXI

A WOMAN RESTS in an apartment in Buenos Aires. Having "lost [her] flair for the art of flight," the narrator of *All My Goodbyes* finds a home in "the atomic number for silicone [and] the properties of butane gas," in which she can "relax and stretch out... as if in a great armchair." She takes solace from copying out the periodic table, which, unlike her broken vase, gives a reliable order to the interactions between elements. And from her armchair—in her state of rest, which is also a form of movement—she remembers herself in place. She tries to find a way to restore the pieces of a puzzle about time and space and pilgrimage and slavery and freedom and love and violence. A puzzle about arrival and departure.

XXII

PERHAPS IT'S BECAUSE I've read in quick succession Olivia Laing's *Crudo* and Deborah Levy's *The Cost of Living*, but it's mid-2018 and, to borrow a word I will later learn from Fiona Wright, I'm feeling unhomed. Reading *Crudo*, I was unnerved to find returned to me my own complicated transition from a life lived alone to one that is shared. Reading *The Cost of Living*, I was troubled to discover how readily I recognised the grim "fairy tale of The Family House," by the way one sentence in particular—"To not feel at home in her family home is the beginning of the bigger story of society and its female discontents"—echoed across the days, weeks, now a year since I finished the book and returned it to the shelf. To make a home and to feel at home. They should be equivalent. Far too often they're not.

Many years ago now, after an extended period away, I returned to my parents' house, that childhood home which for Bachelard incubates all subsequent cosmic dreaming. I felt wrung out and anxious, I was unable to settle. My parents had prepared two adjoining rooms for me—a sort of bedsit—a place where I might rest and slowly regain my strength.

But I was struggling. In those first weeks, I kept to that provisional bedsit, trying and failing to imagine a future for myself, to picture a time beyond this cup of tea, this afternoon nap, this twilight hour when the lamps should be lit. I couldn't see a future time, but I found that I could imagine a place. Not an expansive place: a room. On the sheet of paper where I had intended to describe a future, I drew floor plans, mapped a fireplace, a hearth rug, a pair of armchairs, an angle-poise lamp. This was a warm room. Its walls were painted a deep taupe: until then, not a shade I naturally would have chosen. This was a room that, even on paper, felt like a home.

That weekend, Dad and I went to the paint shop and asked them to mix a colour to match the one I had imagined. We painted the walls, trimming the window frames and the picture rails in a slightly darker enamel. I loved those newly painted rooms and began to feel restored. Now that I think of it, it was in those rooms that I first read Iain Sinclair and the story of his shoes. It was also there that I read Bachelard's *Poetics of Reverie*, and, during one of Melbourne's rare earthquakes, Sebald's *The Rings of Saturn*.

My parents have always hated the colour of those rooms—which are now collectively, colloquially called "the red room" after the lounge suite I also left behind—but they've kept them that way and I like to sit there when I visit. I've grown used to being the only one who feels at home there. I don't mind. But lately, while my parents have been away, Ali and I have been house-sitting—or, more properly, cat-sitting. Ali often returns from work before me and I've learned to look for him first in the red room where, he says, he feels most at home.

XXIII

IN HER ESSAY 'Alternative Routes,' Valeria Luiselli describes attending a conference at which "two experts were discussing the Portuguese term *saudade*." The first expert, Luiselli recalls, "argued that *saudade* is one of those untranslatable words which can only be understood by those who love, experience pleasure and suffer in Portuguese." The other, she goes on, insisted that "if you are not a lusophone... you have no right to borrow *saudade*." "But then," Luiselli asks, "why not just steal the word?"

In spite of its notorious resistance to translation, *saudade* has taken up (nostalgic, melancholic, sorrowful) residence in non-lusophone literatures. Luiselli, who writes in Spanish and English, is attracted to "the constellation of possible meanings" of the word, and she inventories the many "alternative routes" towards an understanding of it. American poet Elizabeth Bishop, for whom *saudade* was "the characteristic Brazilian longing or nostalgia," associated it with the homesickness that inflects much of her own poetry. Italian novelist Antonio Tabucchi, whose works famously capture the spirit of *saudade*, described it as a "continual malaise," "the condition of a subject who finds himself in a state of lack." And according to Australian musician Nick Cave, the word (which he likens to Spanish poet Federico García Lorca's *duende*) embodies "an inexplicable longing, an unnamed and enigmatic yearning of the soul... [which] is the breeding ground for the sad song, for the love song. *Saudade* is the desire to be transported from darkness into light, to be touched by the hand of that which is not of this world." Thus, it suggests a longing for something forever just out of reach: a home in the world, a whole sense of self, love and a lit road leading out of the dark.

The search, in non-lusophone literatures, for the word's elusive meaning finds an echo in the search for a lost place, which illuminates Suneeta Peres da Costa's lyrical novella *Saudade*. Written in English and set in Angola in the lead-up to the War of Independence, the book is narrated by a young woman of Goan descent who comes of age alongside the African nation. The condition of *saudade* is first embodied in the character of Miguel, the narrator's boyfriend and the son of peasants who moved to Angola from the Azores in the hope of a better life. A foreman at a shipwright's factory, Miguel is a devotee of Fernando Pessoa ("the personification of *saudade*," according to Luiselli). He reads Joseph Conrad's *Heart of Darkness* in order to improve his English and describes "the poet Arthur Rimbaud [as] a mercenary who had come to Africa and got into the illegal arms trade." In the character of Miguel—as in so many aspects of this novella—colonial networks are described via the connections they forge between people and places as much as they are by the people and places they render, irreparably, asunder. Via the figures of Pessoa, Conrad, and Rimbaud, an alliance is drawn between militarism, European trade (with its interests in South Africa, the Congo and Ethiopia), and the literature of Empire. Via Miguel and his family, the dislocations set in motion by trade and Empire are revealed to be irreversible. Having abandoned their home in the Azores, and in the face of impending Angolan independence, this family is made permanently homeless. They cannot stay in Angola, but they do not know "how to return to a life they [have] forgotten, to farms that had been abandoned or long since lain fallow." Thus, as the narrator comes to understand him, Miguel is "full of sadness, a saudade—a lostness, a feeling of not having a place in the world."

Historical accounts of *saudade* often associate it with the Portuguese Discoveries, the expansion of Empire and the subsequent trade in slaves between Africa, South America, and Asia. In one of her alternative routes towards an understanding of the term, Luiselli notes that "[i]t's possible... it was the name of a Portuguese ship, the *São Daede*, which, in 1497, preceded Vasco da Gama in the exploration of the Indian Ocean." In Portugal the condition is associated with the feelings of loss and nostalgia experienced by fifteenth century sailors—many of whom never returned—and the families they left behind. Pessoa's *saudade* is frequently expressed in *The Book of Disquiet* via recourse to ocean voyages and shipwreck. "I am," writes his alter-ego, Bernardo Soares, "the shipwreck of my own wanderings." And later, of Lisbon: "I love you as ships passing one another must love, feeling an unaccountable nostalgia in their passing." So it seems that the loss of a beloved place, or at least the inability to be at home in a place except mournfully, and in passing, is intrinsic to the Portuguese experience of *saudade*.

What Peres da Costa captures in her novella are the many ways in which this loss plays out along the lingering alternative (trade) routes of the Portuguese Empire. In his "lostness," Miguel is an "orphan of Empire." So too is Caetano, the servant who, as a small boy, came from Mozambique to live with the narrator and her family and who will eventually die fighting in the Civil War. Likewise, the narrator herself is sent by her mother to Goa, where she adopts a new name, Saudade, after Angola is granted independence. This occurs following the suicide of her father, a labour lawyer with the Ministry of the Interior: the description of the bullet wound in his forehead, "red and large as a carnation in full bloom", is surely a reference to the 1974 Carnation Revolution in Lisbon which eventually led to the withdrawal of Portugal from Angola and its other African colonies. Thus, as a result of the combined forces of colonisation, struggles for liberation, and independence, each of these characters somehow loses a sense of their place in the world.

Peres da Costa draws direct comparisons between her characters: Miguel, born in Portugal; Caetano, born to a Mozambiquan mother and abandoned by his Dutch father; and the narrator, born in Angola, whose parents migrated from Goa to grow rich in the Portuguese colony. But she is careful not to reduce their different degrees of displacement. Caetano, observes the narrator, "was doubly orphaned, with family on the other side of the continent, in Mozambique, which had already become independent." Miguel's "lostness" is, in part, a symptom of his failure to recognise the importance of colonial networks, and the particular geography they describe. An admirer of the anti-colonial leader Amícal Cabral, Miguel "had aspirations to study agronomy. He boasted that he wanted to change lives by taking new farming practices to the poor in Africa, in India. The way he talked of these places, it seemed they were distant—rather than an extension of the very earth on which we stood."

The narrator, in comparison, recognises the extension of Angola towards Mozambique, Portugal, Goa, and beyond. When she and her family move from Benguela to the capital, Luanda, she discovers that the city's streets—the names of which she recites "as Galileo might have recited the relation of the earth to the sun"—are "set out on the same grid as Lisbon, being a mirror of the colonial imaginary." As she describes it, Luanda is a hive of Empire. The market is crowded with traders from Saudi Arabia, the Antilles, and Guinea. Her teachers and friends hail from South Africa, Madeira, the Azores, and mainland Portugal. Her ear is attuned to the sounds of Portuguese, Creole, Konkani, and Kimbundu. And as she grows she comes to understand: that "Konkani was a tongue that... belonged to a people from whom I was... descended"; that in Creole a man could give "voice to a private thought, derisive or mocking, one that he in any case did not care to share with me"; and that, for Ifigênia (the household maid), Kimbundu "might be the language, as I might be the source, of some of [her] plaints and grievances." Well into her childhood, the narrator herself resists "any language that had been taught me," preferring one "of my own improvisation." The streets of Luanda might have been written over by the Lisbon grid. Portuguese and South African soldiers might police those neighbourhoods as agitation for Angolan independence increases. But language remains a potential site of resistance.

Yet language is slippery, as we've seen when it comes to translating the meaning and experience of *saudade*. Part of the lostness associated with Empire is the extent to which colonisation empties the known world of meaning and renders everyone homeless—coloniser as well as colonised—albeit to unequal degrees and with horrifyingly unequal effects. *Saudade* opens with an epigraph from Simone Weil's *Gravity and Grace*, which is concerned with desire, the imagination and movement towards the future. Elsewhere in the same fragment, entitled 'Love,' Weil notes that "[c]ontact with the sword causes the same defilement whether it be through the handle or the point." Although Peres da Costa never trivialises the suffering particular to slaves and indentured labourers, or to the Angolan population colonised by the Portuguese, there is a clear sense throughout her novella that everyone dislocated as a result of Empire suffers a variety of *saudade*. For the narrator, home (in word and imagination) has become an historical curiosity, an antiquated *Terra Australis Incognita*. As a child, she "wondered what home may mean and what different routes one might take to get there." As a young woman, having arrived in Bombay, she finds herself in a "*terra incognita* which I hesitated to call home." Away from Angola, "returned" to Goa even though she has never before been there, the narrator believes that "my destiny was unwritten, a *tabula rasa* all over again," as it had been when she was a child, when her "mind and body were like a *tabula rasa* on which much would be written, even if later I might want it all to be erased."

But is such erasure, a return to the *tabula rasa*, really possible? That the narrator adopts the name Saudade upon her arrival to India suggests not. A Portuguese word notoriously resistant to translation, one deeply associated with the expansion of the Portuguese Empire and which she has defined as "a feeling of not having a place in the world," Saudade carries her homelessness with her to her father's people. Less a *tabula rasa*, then, than a layering, perhaps. Peres da Costa, who was born in Australia to parents of Goan descent, is alive to the palimpsestic writing over of colonial sites and their histories. In her novella, the teenage narrator composes "an alternative biography of Vasco da Gama," in which she overscores "the navigational feats of da Gama's life culminating in the discovery of the trade route to India," and "all the spoils that had resulted from da Gama's first and second voyages—cinnamon, cloves, peppercorns, gold, and, of course, slaves," with "all the acts of terror and brutality which da Gama meted out to the Muslim pilgrims and traders whom he met with in the Arabian Sea and upon arrival on the coast of the Hindus of Calicut." Like this alternative biography, *Saudade* can be read as an alternative route towards understanding the untranslatable sadness of a lost empire.

XXIV

I READ BEVERLEY FARMER'S *A Body of Water* and plant a Virginia creeper in the back garden. I plant it against the shed wall where I can see it through the study window.

I read Deborah Levy's *The Cost of Living* and become convinced that I need a shed to write in. Ali and I share the study. Mostly, our system works—we keep quite different hours—but other times, it really doesn't. I need complete silence. Writing, I need to separate myself from the sounds and the smells and the sights that immediately surround me. Briefly, I think of moving my Danish teak desk into our shed. But there are no windows there, no electricity, barely a concrete floor. What there are, are glossy redbacks and in every corner the old skins of unusually large huntsman spiders, left behind by the moult. So instead, when the neighbours put out a small, paint-spattered table on their nature strip, I bring it inside before the rain. Later, Ali makes space for it in the bedroom between the window and the wardrobe. I fill a cracked mug with HB pencils. In the top left corner, I leave John Berger's *Selected Essays* and a stack of gridded notebooks. I close the door. Ready for work.

I read Olivia Laing's *Crudo* and immediately deactivate my Twitter account. For ten days I feel uncommonly free. Then I remember that I get work via Twitter, and that a world without chatter is a luxury I can't afford.

XXV

WHAT IF IT IS BETTER to remain silent than to speak? This is one of the questions that has been troubling me as I re-read Welsh author Cynan Jones' novels *The Long Dry*, *Everything I Found on the Beach*, *The Dig*, and *Cove*. What is the purpose of putting pen to paper, of muddying the clean page?

Purpose is at the heart of Jones' work: the need for it, the terrible want for it when it's missing. His novels are peopled with farmers and fishermen, men and women who have inherited "a sureness of purpose [that] can only come from having a defined role and not questioning it." Others amongst his characters—badger baiters, drug runners—also have a defined role, but lack the "sureness of purpose" that, for Jones, is intimately associated with responsibility and respect (for people, animals, the land). These men are, to borrow Jones' term, "instruments" of some larger and even more brutal system, one characterised by factory farming and the horrific waste of meat (which is to say, the waste of life) associated with it: "The supermarkets, for example, would want lamb chops, so [the abattoir would] extract the chops and send them on down to the packing line and the rest of the sheep would be tossed, and the dye thrown on it." This web of quotas and bureaucratic regulations disadvantages small farms, giving "the grant people" the power to make decisions about land that does not belong to them, and to which they have no deep connection. It is a system that depends on the exploitation of migrant labour which, under the guise of freedom of movement, transplants desperate Polish farmers to ghettos on the Welsh coast, in the process rendering them beholden to agencies that keep them trapped, fearful, and ineligible for the benefits that should be their due. Ultimately, this is a system that seeks to devolve purpose, decision-making, and responsibility away from the one who acts, to make them believe they are powerless in the face of some nebulous other: the free market, the European Union—Jones puts paid to the lie that free movement benefits everyone equally. "There's four walls round all of us and some screw who pushes a tray through the door," says Stringer, one of the criminals in *Everything I Found on the Beach*. This is a system that, if we let it, would make instruments of us all.

What prevents one from becoming an instrument is a sense of purpose, acknowledgement of the consequences of one's actions and the acceptance of associated responsibility. In *The Dig*, Daniel, a sheep farmer made wretched by grief and exhaustion, nevertheless retains "a feeling of strength—of a reserve of strength; like he could give more, whether tired or not, that this thing is of purpose utmost." Likewise, of one of the protagonists in *Everything I Found on the Beach*, Jones writes:

> That was a very strong thing in Hold: his belief that a thing should not die nor be hurt without purpose. ... Though he fished and shot, this was for a purpose and that he was engineer of the hurt inevitable he felt with great responsibility and that was a great driving force in him. It gave him a respect for life and for the right of things to exist. He felt we had come too far from this.

Hold's belief in purpose and responsibility is juxtaposed with the thoughtless slaughter at the abattoir where Grzegorz and other Polish migrants are employed according to an arrangement reminiscent of indentured labour. Like Hold, Grzegorz has inherited a responsibility—what he describes as a "gratefulness"—to the animal that is killed for food:

> The waste [at the abattoir] was difficult to accept. He thought woefully of how his grandparents would be horrified by the wasteful policies of the place, of the perfectly good meat that was thrown away here. ... Grzegorz thought of the animals butchered in the old kitchen, the pig hanging from its sinews by the big iron hooks and his grandfather's saw cutting down through the ribs, the collected pudding of the blood, the rich, powerful smell of the fresh offal on the woodfired stove. 'This gratefulness to an animal,' he thought, 'is what's gone here. There is a sorrow for it, as there always is, but it is without gratefulness and eventually you just go numb to it. It's the way you have to feel about crowds of people, about strangers. You can't care for them. You can't let yourself. There's too many of them.'

This alignment of the treatment of animals with the treatment of human beings is a common thread in Jones' work. In *Everything I Found on the Beach*, it unfolds via the portrayal of cattle going to slaughter and the instrumentalisation of a desperate man like Grzegorz, who is also "herded like cattle"—first by the agency to which he is bound, then by the drug runners he works for in an attempt to buy his freedom. In *The Dig*, this alignment is articulated in the subtle, symbolic association of the novel's protagonists with other animals. Daniel becomes associated with a black lamb he tries to revive when superstition requires that it be sacrificed "should the Devil come." And, at the end of that novel, the badger-baiter's experience is mirrored in the badger's own terror and confusion of being trapped. In *The Long Dry*, it is the land and those who live on it that come to reflect each other. The earth is dry and, like the marriage at the centre of the novel, "the flowering is over now."

XXVI

WHEN I QUESTION whether it is better to remain silent than to speak, I am thinking of my own purpose in writing, not Cynan Jones'. It may be that this question is prompted by the difficulties associated with writing about work that is self-contained. Like much prose that leans towards the allegorical, Jones' novels seem to be complete in and of themselves.

I could speak of omens, portents, superstitions. Of talismans against the evil eye which are unsettling because they give life to an evil we need protecting from; of a wren's feather, which according to Celtic legend guards against lightning: lightning, which "*is not the strike. It is the local effect of the strike.*" Of swallows and spider crabs that arrive "strangely early"—a local effect of climate change? And of geomagnetic storms that trigger epileptic fits, strokes, and heart attacks, that cause "the electric things" in our bodies to go "wrong," that render the local world dry but which "experts" refuse to acknowledge are connected to "the sudden change of things."

I could speak of attachment to place, the ancient rhythms of life and work on the land: "The hold of the land on the people who grew up here. The hold of a meaningful place." A hold that can also feel like a trap. There are "place[s that] can remember," their histories inscribed on the shape of the land, the division of its fields. There are generations of shearers whose bodies, via the inheritance of repeated movements, are "made only for this purpose." There are moments when, during the lambing season for instance, while assisting a sheep at labour, Daniel understands his connection to those who have done this before him—"the ancientness of this thing he does, that he could be a man of any age"—as well as his connection to the ewe herself:

> There is an understood geography, familiar and mammal, as if some far back thing guides his hands about the lamb inside her, understands the building of the baby, this thing he does, which could be repellent, comfortable to him somehow, the warmth, the balloon warm and lipid. It is only visually there is shame. The fluids and motherly efforts are beyond that, too ancient for shame, and he understands a great and vital force at work, equanimical with his instinct and assured.

I could speak of life—that vital force in all of us. But equally, I could speak of the instinct toward violence; of brutality, and the deliberate, "articulate cruelty" of men like the badger-baiter, who brings "a sense of harmfulness" wherever he goes. Men who nurture a hate for people and other animals they cast as weak, but who "smash... the lower jaw" of a badger "with a spade to give the dogs a chance." Others who "keep [men like Grzegorz] constantly down. ... Keep you scared. So you just get on and follow the line. Just like those stupid obedient cows who wander along the line into the stun, as if it was the only way their life would ever have gone."

But also, always, I could speak of the instinct to protect and to relieve suffering. An instinct that is charged with a violence of its own. There are the boys who come upon a desperate, dying rabbit and determine to "finish it off": "And the boy didn't show anything but inside he asked the rabbit if it was alright to do this and the rabbit's eye just half-closed in defeat, very slowly."

And so, I could speak of love. Love of land, of life, human and animal. Love that, in Hold, is bound up with "a great sense of guilt at anything he took for himself. It was his will to provide without taking. It was, in a way, a form of self-harm." Love that takes responsibility for the loved one. Shipwrecked, struck by lightning and adrift at sea, the protagonist of *Cove* is determined to make land for love of his wife and unborn child: "He felt a massive responsibility. He wanted to make sure she knew how to reset the pilot light on the boiler." Never, in Jones' work, is love uncomplicated. It requires control—of anger and of desire, both of which can be dangerous. And when the loved one is lost, when the role one has assumed comes under question, then love can lead to a desire to forfeit all purpose and responsibility. Daniel feels "a great want… to suffer some unpassable collision so that he could just lie down." The protagonist of *The Long Dry* dreams guiltily of "[a] crisis, that would reiterate the importance of life and of reaping happily from it what you could."

I could speak of these things—as I think of them while reading Cynan Jones—but I can't help asking myself what the purpose of such talk would be. There is much to say—about portentous changes in weather and shifts in animal migrations, about place, about the vital forces of life, love, violence—and Jones has said it. His spare, lyrical prose (which has been compared by successive reviewers to that of Ernest Hemingway, Cormac McCarthy, John Steinbeck, the young Ian McEwan, and others) shuns any kind of elaboration.

And yet, I elaborate. As if, like one of Jones' characters, I am following some "primal instinct"—an instinct to make land, to protect the sick, or to brutalise the weak. An instinct to fulfil a role and accept its purpose. I make the decision to speak.

XXVII

READING AN AUTHOR'S BODY OF WORK, I regard each individual narrative as part of a larger whole. This approach seeks out the points of connection between each book and in these connections discovers a consolidation of allusion and theme, a slow accretion of meaning, tone, atmosphere. In the case of Cynan Jones, I have been drawn to instances of love and violence, to the hold of place and the desire to break free of it.

But reading Jones in this way has also led me to question my approach, to become aware of the ways in which it is, perhaps, artificial. I find myself listening more closely to some works than to others, seeking out one allusion at the expense of another. The optimism of *Cove*, for instance, is lost to this analysis. A concentrated reading might give force to the body of work, but what does it do to an individual narrative? What is, to borrow Jones' phrase, "the local effect" of such a comprehensive approach?

In each of Jones' narratives there is brutality, but this brutality finds its most extreme expression in *The Dig*. Here, Jones takes his description of the cruelty of badger-baiting well beyond what is comfortable and on to the outer limits of what is bearable for the reader. Read on its own, *The Dig* is a meditation upon violence and loss. But read in concert, with *Everything I Found on the Beach* in particular, its violence and loss become part of a larger allegorical project that aligns the treatment of human beings and other animals to a deeply political end. *The Dig* opens with a graphic description of the dead body of a brutalised badger and a badger-baiter who refuses to touch it because that would give the creature a kind of "reverence." Following a chronological rereading of Jones' work, by the time I reached this point it was difficult to ignore the association of the badger with the cattle sent to slaughter in *Everything I Found on the Beach*, let alone the association of the cattle with men like Grzegorz and Hold, Daniel in *The Dig*, the husband and wife of *The Long Dry*, even the badger-baiter himself, who are, in their own ways, trapped and made brutal and trying to hold to their purposes in the face of the desperate temptation to give in, to lie down, to rest—which in Jones' fiction is always associated with a kind of death.

It is the concentration of this brutality—brought to the limit of what is bearable—that is at the root of the question with which I began. When is it better to remain silent than to speak? To what end do we speak of men's "articulate cruelty"? One answer is to be found in Jones' body of work, in its intersecting associations. Speaking of one form of cruelty illuminates another. Like cattle sent to slaughter, human beings are corralled by agencies, banks, bureaucratic "grant people." The choice—if there is one—is not between life and death, between the violent death of a baited badger and the natural death of a black lamb; as the protagonist of *The Long Dry* tells it, "He'd seen a lot of things die, and none of them beautifully." But there might still be a choice between a life (and death) lived with or without purpose. Cynan Jones leaves many things unspoken, and in his narratives many secrets are kept. But his novels—read singly or in concert—are everywhere shaped by the "belief that a thing should not die nor be hurt without purpose." On the page and elsewhere, we might find, still, "a respect for life and for the right of things to exist."

XXVIII

I READ Robert Macfarlane's *The Wild Places* and take the train from Edinburgh, where I've been working, to Rannoch Moor. "Many know the Moor," Macfarlane writes, "but relatively few enter it, for it is vast and trackless and has a reputation for hostility at all times of the year." I've spent the last two months crisscrossing the city, helping to coordinate the installation of the visual arts programme of the Edinburgh International Festival. I'm exhausted from lugging AV equipment between locations, from negotiating with artists and gallerists and installation crews, from trying to avoid the "free hugs" that are being meted out along the Royal Mile as a part of Fringe. I'm looking forward to a "vast and trackless" space. Instead, I find the cast and crew of *Harry Potter*, there to film the train journey to Hogwarts. It was here on "the mystical Rannoch Moor," I later read on the Visit Scotland website, "where Death Eaters board the train in the movie *Harry Potter and the Deathly Hallows: Part 1*."

But a week later, after the Death Eaters have moved on, after a bath and a peaty whiskey alone by the fire, after, finally, quiet and a good night's sleep, I walk into the Moor. It's drizzling, but I leave the hood of my jacket down so I can listen. I wish I could leave behind the sound of my footsteps. I'm so focussed on silencing the rustle of my waterproof that I almost miss the doe standing still a few meters ahead. I watch her, she watches me and I suddenly remember another journey, years ago, crossing Victoria's Alpine National Park *en route* to Mount Bulla. It was off-season;

I had the road to myself and I reached the crest of Mount Hotham in a brilliantly violet dusk. When, out of habit, I checked the rear view mirror, my eyes met those of a rabbit, standing by the roadside, as startled by my passing as I was at being seen. It wasn't a comfortable encounter. We stayed like that, our eyes meeting, until the road curved and I was forced to look ahead. I carried on to Bulla, but I left a sense of trespass in my wake.

I go to the Natural History Museum in London to see a temporary display: *Scott's Last Expedition*. There, I read about the Northern Party: the six men who, from January to October 1912, with only six weeks' supplies, became stranded and were forced to overwinter in an ice cave they dug at Evans Cove. All of them survived. Afterwards, I can't stop thinking about these parallel narratives: the death of Scott and all the members of his polar party, the stubborn lives of Victor Campbell, George Murray Levick, Raymond Priestley, George Abbott, Frank Browning, and Harry Dickason. I read what more I can on the Northern Party. I think about finding my way to Antarctica. But I hate gale-force winds, and I've heard rumours of the kind of "training" required for those who intend to accompany a scientific expedition—training that includes prolonged submersion in icy water—and whether or not these rumours are true, we've already established that I'm cowardly when it comes to personal comfort (remember the blood-tarnished eye of a wounded fish, redbacks and the husks of huntsman spiders). So I go to the archive instead.

I spend as long as I can spare—longer, really—in Cambridge. Every morning, I walk from my B&B overlooking Parker's Piece to the Scott Polar Research Archive. I sit down at the desk I've booked (one of only two), don the white gloves, read the journals that Campbell and his party kept during their time at Evans Cove. March 1st: "If there is no sign of the ship this morning I must start killing seals for the winter." April 28th: "No seals." May 7th:

"Today we are snowed in. L and B skinning and cutting up penguins in the outer galley while P and D have tunnelled out a shaft through the drift. P luckily has the old journal with him and reads aloud to us which is very interesting and brings everything back to us. L reads us a chapter of *David Copperfield* so altogether our evenings pass very pleasantly."

The further I read, the closer Campbell's writing becomes, the more his pages are smudged with blood and blubber. On one page, a perfect blackened fingerprint. I think of him building a fire out of seal bones, seaweed, and blubber. I think of him trying to preserve the matches, until there's enough for only one hour of light a day, and sometimes not even that. Still, he writes. On the days when the cave remains unlit, unheated, Campbell's writing is large and slanted, the script of a small child just learning to hold the pen.

In the archive, at 11AM precisely and again at 3PM, a bell rings. Everyone leaves what they are doing, stands and moves out of the room. These breaks are compulsory. At first I resent being forced to leave the snow cave. Eventually, I look forward to the bell as one might a break in the weather. The archivist locks the door behind us and we tramp into the library, where tea and coffee are served on a trolley. There we find other people, researchers working in other parts of the building. I talk to one man who, in the 1970s, was stranded in Antarctica for two years. The teacup feels especially warm between my hands.

I read and re-read and read again W.G. Sebald: *Vertigo, The Emigrants, The Rings of Saturn, Austerlitz*. Eventually, I make the pilgrimage to Suffolk. To get there, I cross the Orwell River and drive past field after muddy field of pigs. *Animal Farm* suddenly makes a different kind of sense. I pass Walnut Tree Farm and think of Roger Deakin. There is a sign at the gate that reads: PRIVATE. Perhaps it's the memory of this that, at the Southwold Sailor's Reading Room, flicking through the Visitors Book and seeing one after another the messages left by other Sebald pilgrims, causes me to flush with shame. I feel that I have finally overstepped. That I have failed to respect the line dividing the work from the private human being who made it.

XXIX

IN THE TITLE STORY of Samanta Schweblin's ferociously good collection, *Mouthful of Birds*, a man buys a small bird for his daughter, Sara, who, at the age of thirteen, has begun to eat only live sparrows. The pet shop from which he makes his purchase includes with it a breeder's pamphlet: "On the back was information about how to care for the bird, and about its reproduction cycles. [It] emphasized the species' need to be in pairs during warm months, and the things one can do to make the years in captivity as pleasant as possible." Standing at the door to Sara's bedroom, looking over the pamphlet with its care instructions, the narrator hears "a brief shriek" which indicates that his daughter is feeding. The inference is clear: this bird will not be captive long.

But others in this collection will be—are—and Schweblin's stories catalogue lives lived in captivity more or (more often) less pleasantly. In 'Toward Happy Civilization,' office workers lacking the correct change for their return train fare to the capital are held captive by the station master and his wife, for whom they become surrogate children bound to work the surrounding fields, to feed the dog, to hunt rabbits for the makeshift family's midday and evening meals. In 'Headlights,' newlywed brides are deserted by their husbands at a women's bathroom on the highway. Bereft, arrested in the moment of abandonment, they gather in the fields, "wailing and plaintive," repeating "the names of their husbands over and over." In 'Rage of Pestilence,' a civil servant travels the border territories to gather census details from "poor communities" who, for their trouble, are "remunerated with food." At one remote village, with a palm full of sugar he releases the population from their indifference to suffering and unleashes upon them "the memory of hunger." And in 'My Brother Walter,' a family's increasing good fortunes appear to depend upon the deep and persistent depression of the narrator's brother. At weekend barbeques, near and extended relations gather around Walter "to cheer him up or keep him company" while taking pains "to talk about more or less superficial subjects, and always optimistically." Walter, meanwhile, caught in the glare of his family's oppressive goodwill, sits wearing "a baleful expression, sadder and sadder all the time."

Weird and often surrealistic, Schweblin's stories render the lives captured in them uncannily familiar, and her blisteringly dark humour illuminates the absurdity of contemporary life. In *Mouthful of Birds*, parents and their children, workers and their supervisors, artists and their audiences struggle within, and against, the confinement of their being in relation to one another. Thus, in a vein that will be familiar to readers of Schweblin's novella, *Fever Dream*, a father crushes the daughter he holds most dear, in the story 'Butterflies.' In 'The Size of Things,' an adult man regresses to infancy in the company of his overbearing mother. In 'On the Steppe,' a childless couple spend their days concocting fertility recipes and their nights hunting in the surrounding wilderness, stalking an unspecified "them," ready with a net to capture "ours." Again, in 'A Great Effort,' a father and his adult son are finally released from their injurious bond by the deft "surgical movement" of a massage therapist.

Work—including the work of art—is a recurring concern of Schweblin's, as it is for Jorge Consiglio and Mariana Dimópulos, all of them Argentines. It is possible to read across Schweblin's stories an argument both for the value of labour and against the alienation of workers from themselves, and (via) that labour. In the remarkable story 'Olingiris,' for instance, women visit "the institute" to salve their trichotillomania against the body of another. Under clinically regulated conditions, a woman lies naked, face down on a cot, while six others "get to work," tweezering the hairs from her legs:

> They hold the tweezers poised over the woman's body, quickly choose a hair, and lower them, open, decisive. They close, pinch, yank. The dark bulb comes out clean and perfect. They study it a second... then go for the next one. Six seagulls' beaks pulling fish from the sea. The hair in the tweezers fills them with pleasure. Some of them do the work to perfection. The whole hair hangs from the tweezers, orphaned and useless. Others struggle a bit with the task and have to try more than once. But nothing deprives them of their pleasure.

The pleasurable work of closing, pinching, yanking elides the actual, paid labour of "the woman on the cot" and "the assistant" who monitors her, making a note of any unwitting tremors, "infractions" that are penalised by docking the prone woman's pay. From the white room, the cot, and "the squeak of the [assistant's] rubber sandals stopping short" as she records another tremor, the narrative shifts first to the biography of the woman on the cot, then to that of the assistant. As children, both were preoccupied with fish. One grew up among fishermen, on the banks of a river susceptible to flood. The other had a passion for the exotic Olingiris but was refused a pet because her mother believed that, in captivity, the fish "would die of sadness." This is the sadness of alienation, which abandons the assistant to the role of captor and the woman on the cot to the mercy of "six seagulls' beaks pulling fish from the sea."

The dehumanising effects of institutionalised work are represented elsewhere in *Mouthful of Birds*, often in relation to animals.

'The Test,' in which the coolly sadistic Mole assesses a job applicant's willingness to do violence, is a particularly caustic example of this. But in other stories, among them 'Towards Happy Civilization,' the value of certain varieties of labour is brought into startling relief. For, although the stranded office workers are held against their will by the station master and his wife, the lives they lead with them are sinisterly comfortable, the food they help to gather and prepare is Grimm-like in its succulence, and the work they do in the surrounding fields is healthy and, at least superficially, fulfilling. As a result, looking back from the departing train after they have finally made their escape, the men cannot help but wonder if the scene they are leaving behind them looks something like the "happy civilization" they believed they were instead moving towards.

Often in Schweblin's imagined universe, conventionally anomalous events illuminate the aberrant nature of the world lived beyond the page. Thus, in 'Mouthful of Birds,' Sara's grotesque feeding habits—her "nose, chin, and both hands... smeared with blood" and her "gigantic mouth arch[ing] and open[ing]" to reveal her "red teeth"—leave her radiant with good health. In contrast, her father compulsively roams the supermarket aisles, subsists largely on canned foods, and begins to wonder "if it was really worth it to fill [his cart] with so much garbage." Similarly, in 'Preserves,' a woman who finds herself prematurely pregnant searches for a way to delay the birth of her daughter. Marvelling at a world in which a person can thaw "a fresh fish that died thirty days ago," she and her husband look for, and discover, a means to "make a small change in the order of events." Such narratives illuminate the extraordinary character of the apparently everyday.

But it is in stories like 'Heads Against Concrete' and 'The Heavy Suitcase of Benavides' that the worlds on and beyond the page collide most savagely. Here, Schweblin considers the problem of art and its industry, which recasts a violent impulse as "the work" in order to turn a profit. 'Heads Against Concrete' chronicles the misadventures of an artist who, as a socially awkward boy, would occasionally vent his frustration by "pound[ing] a person's head against concrete." On one such occasion he experienced an "illumination," which led him instead to paint "in extreme close-up" a pounded head in lieu of the physical act of violence. Now, still socially awkward, the narrator's paintings have brought him considerable success, including "a loft in downtown Buenos Aires" and a gallerist who visits every day to offer words of encouragement: "You're a mega-genius. A me-ga ge-nius." Naturally, the artist suffers a relapse, and the art industry attempts to turn this, too, to profit.

Likewise, in 'The Heavy Suitcase of Benavides,' when a man who has murdered his wife and stuffed her body into a suitcase shows his psychiatrist what he has done, he is lauded as an artist, not a criminal, and "the work" is celebrated as "truly beautiful." Schweblin's razor-sharp wit cuts through the ludicrous discourse of the contemporary art market, as a curator and his team of handlers descend upon the suitcase and prepare it for a sycophantic audience:

> "I'm just a curator, my part is minimal. The important thing here is the work, *Violence*, understand?"
>
> "My wife."
>
> "No, Benavides, believe me, I know marketing and that won't work. The title is *Violence*."
>
> ...
>
> "But I killed her..."
>
> "Yes, Benavides, yes. We know it was you, no one is going to take that away from you. ... Trust us with this, you'll just see how you take your place among the stars."

In both stories, these men become alienated from their natural—if criminal—acts by an industry that sees in the real only a form of representation. When the artist of 'Heads Against Concrete' pounds the skull of a man into one of his own canvases, an interviewer asks about the "aesthetic intention" of this act. And Benavides, who finally accepts "the work" of *Violence* and his place among the stars, is rewarded by witnessing "a chasm open... in front of him [that] separates him from the rest of humanity."

In 'The Heavy Suitcase of Benavides,' art is conceived of as "anxiety contained." But, like the palm full of sugar proffered by the well-meaning civil servant in 'A Rage of Pestilence,' Schweblin's stories unleash that anxiety and turn it to radical effect. *Mouthful of Birds* conveys the real violence of the world beyond the page: in one person's captive relation to another, at work, and via the work of art.

XXX

AT HOME WITH BRONCHITIS, I play endless games of Patience (none of which come out) and read the back catalogues of Anita Brookner and Barbara Pym. I've just reached the part in Brookner's *A Start in Life* when the protagonist, Ruth Weiss, who has travelled to France to visit the settings of Balzac's novels—"ground that might yield up secrets," that might lead her to "read the texts in a new and enlightened way"—realises that the worlds dreamed on and beyond the page do not always align, when Ali calls. Some of his poems are on the secondary school curriculum this year, and he's interstate talking to teachers about them. He's just spent an hour speaking about parataxis, poetry, and ideology. Afterwards, he tells me, one teacher in the audience declared, angrily, that "whether he likes it or not" they will use his poems to illustrate an identity position to which he doesn't hold. Now he's waiting for a train to take him into the centre of the city he's visiting. Do I want anything? he asks. If he comes across a good bookshop, I reply, please bring home some more Anita Brookner.

XXXI

Some books—my favourite sort—I like to read inside-out. I want to excavate a deep-topography of the narrative via others that have inspired it and from which it draws breath. To that end, I keep an index card and an HB pencil handy. I note down references to texts or authors, phrases or images that persistently recur. I'm not an underliner, preferring when I re-read to do so with a fresh eye, but occasionally, when the need is great I will buy another edition of a book, which I then mark up freely. So, when I open my second copy of W.G. Sebald's *The Emigrants* to a page at random, I rediscover Paul Bereyter: "He read and read—Altenberg, Trakl, Wittgenstein, Friedell, Hasenclever, Toller, Tucholsky, Klaus Mann, Ossietsky, Benjamin, Koestler and Zweig: almost all of them writers who had taken their own lives or had been close to doing so." In my copy of Teju Cole's *Blind Spot*, I find an index card covered on both sides with names and titles, among them: *Sans Soleil*, Edna O'Brien, *Iliad*, Caravaggio, Emily Dickinson, Nadia Tuéni, Holmes & Watson & *Go Tell It on the Mountain*, Merleau-Ponty, *Slavers Throwing Overboard the Dead and Dying*, John Coltrane. And, in Chloe Aridjis' *Asunder*, on a page marked with a postcard reproduction of Velásquez's *Rokeby Venus*, I'm reminded that "craquelure grants a painting its history, its authenticity, a whole topography the painter himself could never have envisioned."

Such books are embedded within particular histories of thought and representation and there is an archival quality to this reading inside-out, which builds an archive of the text, and documents the experience of reading and re-reading it. On the bookshelves in the study—although it disrupts the otherwise strict alphabetical order—I keep Conrad, Kafka, Nabokov, and Wittgenstein alongside Sebald. Reading *Blind Spot*, I wish we kept a Bible in the house. I pause frequently, regardless, to pull down from the shelf John Berger's *Understanding a Photograph*, to listen to Brahms, to look for Emily Dickinson's *Complete Poems*, which isn't where it should be. (I find it, eventually, in a pile Ali has gathered together—with Auden's *Collected Shorter Poems*, Jorie Graham's *Place*, John Berryman's *77 Dream Songs*, and H.D.'s *Collected Poems 1912-1944*—an archive to which I don't yet have the key.)

Such books—Sebald's, Cole's—are also deeply embedded in particular places. I have made the requisite pilgrimage to Suffolk—following in the footsteps of the narrator of *The Rings of Saturn* as well as those who have come after him—and I'm still troubled by the journey. I re-read *Vertigo* and *The Emigrants* with a Hallwag map of Europe's Alpine territories spread out before me. I use a Post-it to mark the world map in *Blind Spot* and flick back to it repeatedly. Often, as befits a narrative tradition preoccupied with time, the spaces of these texts are ghosted by the other people who have passed through, and the events that have taken place in them. These books are palimpsestic. I'm thinking of Cole's overlayering of narratives in *Blind Spot*: of the intersection, for instance, at a crossroads on the Gemmipass, of Cole with his camera, Sherlock Holmes, Dr. Watson, Moriarty, and James Baldwin. They are also topographical. I'm thinking, too, of Sebald's "long topographical litany": those mountains, rivers, lakes and seas, those ruined cities and sites of abandoned industry, those cloistered reading rooms to which he and his characters compulsively return.

It is commonplace, especially it seems to me when actual feeling is involved, to dismiss the affect of literature and other artforms. That's just a film, a novel, a play, people say: Why do you care?

It's not real. At best one might be permitted to experience emotion in response to art if it is framed as catharsis. However this, too, has a quarantining effect; it fortifies the boundary between art and the so-called real world. But the books and the writers I speak of here cannot be quarantined so easily.

There is an early essay of Berger's, 'Drawing,' that I have returned to again and again since I first read it, almost twenty years ago now. As its title suggests, it is an essay about drawing—specifically about working drawings, which for Berger are "autobiographical record[s] of one's discovery of an event" as opposed to a "finished work [which is] an attempt to construct an event in itself." Berger argues that "it is the act of drawing that forces the artist to look at the object in front of him," and in my own reading of his essay I have come to think of the act of writing as a comparable way of looking at the world. Looking from the life model to the paper before him, Berger emphasises the real space of the page and the effect of making a mark upon it:

> I now began to see the white surface of the paper, on which I was going to draw, in a different way. From being a clean flat page it became an empty space. Its whiteness became an area of limitless, opaque light, possible to move through but not to see through. I knew that when I drew a line on it—or *through* it—I should have to control the line, not like the driver of a car, on one plane: but like a pilot in the air; movement in all three dimensions being possible.

I cannot overstate the feeling of vertigo triggered by the possibility of moving *through* the page in *all three dimensions*. It is a feeling akin to reading Sebald and Cole; although I wonder if the pages they inhabit were ever empty to begin with. The palimpsestic nature of their work would suggest perhaps not, being as they are already peopled, by Wittgenstein and Benjamin, by Holmes and Baldwin, and already placed, on the Gemmipass and other Alpine territories. But, at heart, these narratives are multiple and three-dimensional. They force the reader to look at the world before them, even when that world is presented "obliquely, tangentially, by reference rather than direct confrontation," as Sebald once described it in an interview with Michael Silverblatt. Books that can be—demand to be—read in this way are inherently terrestrial: they create a multi-dimensional world via the page that has the potential to intervene in the so-called real world beyond it.

XXXII

I'M TEMPTED TO SAY that no other book I've read recently exists fully in three dimensions more than Valeria Luiselli's extraordinary epic novel, *Lost Children Archive*. Certainly I'm at a loss to think of one that does, especially in response to continually unfolding events. And although critics have repeatedly coupled Luiselli's name with Sebald's, as they have done Cole's, a distinction must be made between this novel and Sebald's oblique, tangential narrative approach. Because here Luiselli confronts "this empty, fucked-up world" directly—ferociously—as well as by reference to the deep, geographical-historical and literary archive written into her narrative.

Lost Children Archive maps a family's road trip from New York City to Cochise County, Arizona, and is narrated in turns by a woman and her ten-year-old step-son (neither of whom, like the woman's husband and her five-year-old daughter, are formally named). This is a vast, centrifugal novel that circles outwards from the family driving southwest through the ruins of late capitalism, towards Apacheria "where the last free peoples on the entire American continent lived before they had to surrender to the white-eyes." It spirals away from the safety of the car towards the tens of thousands of undocumented children from Mexico and the Northern Triangle (Guatemala, El Salvador, and Honduras) who are moving north, hoping to reach the US-Mexico border. As he drives, the woman's husband tells the two children stories of Chief Cochise, Geronimo, and the Eagle Warriors, "a band of Apache children... [who] lived in a place called Echo Canyon, a place where the echoes are so loud and clear that even if you whisper, your voice comes right back to you, crisp." Between these stories and the games the boy and the girl elaborate from them ("[L]et's steal the white cows, the white, the white-eyes' cows!"), between audio books and music playlists, between Cormac McCarthy's *The Road* and David Bowie's 'Space Oddity' (both of which echo throughout the novel), the woman scans the radio whenever there's a signal, searching for news of the children moving north:

> I think of all those children, undocumented, who cross Mexico in the hands of a coyote, riding atop train cars, trying to not fall off, to not fall into the hands of migration authorities, or into the hands of drug lords who would enslave them in poppy fields, if they don't kill them. If they make it all the way to the US border, they try to turn themselves in, but if they don't find a Border Patrol officer, the children walk into the desert.

The woman's concern for these undocumented children is at once general and specific. Back in New York, she had been helping another woman, Manuela, whose two daughters made the perilous journey north from Mexico. During the drive southwest, the narrator receives word that the girls have disappeared prior to their removal: as Luiselli outlines in her essay *Tell Me How It Ends*, children from Mexico are subject to immediate deportation under United States law and refused "temporary shelter, ... contact with parents or relatives in the U.S., and... [the] right to a formal hearing in court where they could defend themselves, legally, against a deportation order."

Luiselli's concern in this novel is likewise general and specific. From the stories of the lost children and the last of the Apache, the novel broadens into more spacious territory, with a deeper and disturbing history. "No one," the woman rages,

> looks at the bigger map, historical and geographical, of a refugee population's migration routes. ... No one thinks of the children arriving here now as refugees of a hemispheric war that extends, at least, from these very mountains [the Appalachians], down the country into the southern US and northern Mexican deserts, sweeping across the Mexican sierras, forests, and southern rain forests into Guatemala, into El Salvador, and all the way to the Celaque Mountains in Honduras. No one thinks of those children as consequences of a historical war that goes back decades. Everyone keeps asking: Which war, where? Why are they here? Why did they come to the United States? What will we do with them? No one is asking: Why did they flee their homes?

In *Lost Children Archive*, Luiselli has composed a bigger map and a longer historical perspective of the routes taken by these child refugees who are "fleeing circumstances of unspeakable abuse and systematic violence, fleeing countries where gangs had become parastates, had usurped power and taken over the rule of law." But this map extends even farther, beyond the migration of Central American children and the immediate war that has forced them to flee. In keeping with the centrifugal logic of the narrative, Luiselli's map circles outwards from the car and the radioed news of children riding La Bestia, the freight trains that run from Tapachula on the Guatemala-Mexico border north toward the United States. It curls outwards again, from La Bestia towards the child crusaders of the thirteenth century, many of whom were sold into slavery; towards the "purchase" and "importation," in the eighteenth century, of "children from the coast of Africa," slaves "who would live longer" and therefore profit slavers more; towards the removal of the Apache from their lands, by train in 1886; towards the relocation by Orphan Train, between 1854 and 1930, of over 200,000 homeless and abandoned children from New York to the western United States, where "[s]ome ended up with good families, which took care of them. Others were taken in as servants or slaves, enduring inhumane living conditions. Sometimes unspeakable abuse."

The ferocity of Luiselli's novel and the energy with which she moves through the page in all three dimensions, composing (to echo Berger) an autofictional record of the discovery of an event and its long history, is fuelled by her work at the federal immigration court in New York City. In 2015, Luiselli began serving as a volunteer translator for unaccompanied child migrants. This experience became the subject of *Tell Me How It Ends: An Essay in Forty Questions*. *Lost Children Archive* echoes this earlier work in the same way as it does so many other texts—*The Road* and 'Space Oddity' but also *Lord of the Flies*, also (in *Elegies for Lost Children*, a text within the text of the novel) "Ezra Pound, Juan Rulfo, T.S. Eliot, Jerzy Andrzejewski, Emily Dickinson, Lázló Krasznahorkai, Rainer Maria Rilke, James Baldwin," also Walt Whitman's 'Passing Stranger,' also the photographs of Man Ray and Sally Mann, and so on and on beyond the literary archive—those texts by which the world may be represented obliquely, tangentially, by reference rather than direct confrontation—to the Migrant Mortality Reports ("Name: ARIZAGA, BABY BOY ... Age: 0 ... Cause of Death: Nonviable") and the map, discovered by the boy in the woman's archive box, which "showed a space, like any map, but in that space there were hundreds of little red dots... [and] I realized the red dots stood for people who had died there, in that exact spot," and the objects "found on migrant trails in the desert" (a toothbrush and toothpaste, a photograph, a telephone)—all of them documents that confront "this empty, fucked-up world" and demand that we look directly at it. Look.

XXXIII

In their concerted composition of a bigger map and a longer historical view, Valeria Luiselli's *Lost Children Archive* and *Tell Me How It Ends* work together in a way reminiscent of other projects that cannot be captured in a single work, or a single genre. I'm thinking, for instance, of Virginia Woolf's essay *Three Guineas* and her novel *The Years*, of Arundhati Roy's essay *Capitalism: A Ghost Story* and her novel *The Ministry of Utmost Happiness*. Towards the conclusion of *Tell Me How It Ends*, Luiselli reflects on the importance of contemporary narration as a way of thinking through (or discovering) unfolding events:

> There are things that can only be understood retrospectively, when many years have passed and the story has ended. In the meantime, while the story continues, the only thing to do is tell it over and over again as it develops, bifurcates, knots around itself. And it must be told, because before anything can be understood, it has to be narrated many times, in many different words and from many different angles, by many different minds.

Luiselli's project incorporates multiple narrations and various perspectives: her own, alongside those of some of the children and their relatives whom she met at the federal immigration court, in *Tell Me How It Ends*; the woman and the boy narrators, and voices from the literary and historical record, in *Lost Children Archive*. But perhaps the most powerful aspect of this project is her insistence upon a narrative approach that confronts the "unaccompanied child migrant crisis" as one part of a long history of child slavery, from the thirteenth century to now, and in which numerous US governments are implicated—a history traceable at least as far back as 1848, when Mexico "sold" Arizona to the United States following its loss in what "Americans call the Mexican-American War and Mexicans call, perhaps more accurately, the American Intervention."

Insisting upon an expansive historical-geographical view, *Lost Children Archive*, in combination with *Tell Me How It Ends*, intervenes in the world beyond the page. It disrupts the current, popular narrative of one deranged president and his wall and documents the insidious actions of successive US administrations, all of them hell-bent on fortifying the border with Mexico while continuing to profit from the sale of arms, the trade in drugs, and no doubt (although Luiselli doesn't specify this), the exploitation of undocumented labour. These actions warrant testimony, variedly and repeatedly. The actions, for example, of the "Carter administration and, perhaps more actively, the Reagan administration [which] funded and provided military resources to the [Salvadoran] government that massacred so many and led many others to exile"; of Bill Clinton, "who laid the first brick in the wall dividing Mexico and the United States, and then pretended it never happened"; of George W. Bush, who in 2008 signed an amendment to the Trafficking Victims Protection Reauthorization Act, which "states that children from countries that share borders with the U.S. can be deported without formal immigration proceedings"; of the Obama administration, which in 2014 "created the priority Juvenile docket", thus reducing from twelve months to twenty-one days the time given to "minors seeking immigration relief" to find legal representation and "imply[ing] that deportation proceedings against them were accelerated by 94 percent"; and the actions of the Mexican government, which (following President Obama's meeting with President Enrique Peña Nieto) introduced the Programa Frontera Sur that includes such "anti-immigrant strategies" as "the notorious Grupos Beta, which, under the guise of a humanitarian aid organization, locates and then reports migrants to immigration officials, who can then 'secure' them—a Mexican euphemism for 'capture and deport'." It goes without saying, but it must be said anyway, that the US State Department "has paid the Mexican government tens of millions of dollars to filter the migration of Central Americans"—much as, in Australia, my own government has paid the Micronesian Republic of Nauru for hosting its "offshore processing facility" for refugees seeking asylum. And as the re-elected Conservative Coalition will continue to do, indefinitely.

Just as Luiselli presents an expansive, multivocal, historical-geographical perspective on the movement of child refugees, she confronts the language used to instil fear of "aliens" ("Kids, a Biblical Plague" declares one newspaper headline) and to normalise the government's defence against them. There is, throughout *Lost Children Archive*, an insistence upon the politics of language, and so it seems apposite that this should be the first novel Luiselli has written in English. Like most Anglophone readers, I imagine, until now I have read Luiselli's work—*Sidewalks, Faces in the Crowd*, and *The Story of My Teeth*—in Christina MacSweeney's beautiful translations from the Spanish. And I was (stupidly) unprepared for the difference it makes to hear Luiselli's voice untranslated. It's a curious difference, one that I still can't quite put my finger on, but which I've come to think of as another of those ways in which *Lost Children Archive* confronts the English-speaking world—specifically the world of US history—directly. A primary example of this confrontation is the attention Luiselli gives to euphemisms—secure, undocumented, illegal, removal, relocation—that "hide, erase, coat" real actions and their consequences; euphemisms that "lead us to tolerate the unacceptable.

And, eventually, to forget." "Against a euphemism," the woman notes, "remembrance. In order to not repeat." And, to aid remembrance, documentation. The creation of an archive.

XXXIV

THE WOMAN IN *Lost Children Archive* is a documentarian. Her husband is a documentarist. The boy aspires to be a documentarianist and addresses his account, composed of a voice recording and Polaroid photographs, to the girl who he fears is too young to remember the journey herself. He explains the difference between their parents' work thus: "a documentarian is like a librarian and a documentarist is like a chemist [or, as the woman defines it, 'an alchemist']. But both of them did basically the same thing: they had to find sounds, record them, store them on tape, and then put them together in a way that they told a story." Despite these similarities in practice, the man and the woman are pulling away from each other, each one following a different narrative thread. The family's drive southwest has been prompted by the man's desire to compose an "inventory of echoes"; to travel to Apacheria and document sounds of "the ghosts of Geronimo and the last Apaches." Back in New York, the woman had embarked upon a project recording the stories of undocumented children and resents having had to leave the city. But as news breaks of more and more children crossing the border and of the disappearance of the daughters of her friend, Manuela, she begins to understand that "the story I need to tell is the one of the children who are missing, those whose voices can no longer be heard because they are, possibly forever, lost." Of course, in accordance with Luiselli's big map and long historical view, these narratives intersect and overlap. But that intersection cannot revive the man and the woman's marriage. As the boy describes it: "One was a documentarian and the other a documentarist, and neither one wanted to give up being who they were."

Documentation—the need for it, the complicated politics of it—is at the core of *Lost Children Archive*. In the trunk of the car, along with their clothes, their recording equipment, and other essentials, the family carries with them seven archival boxes. "They would travel with us, like an appendix of us," says the woman. "I numbered them carefully with a black marker. Boxes I through IV were my husband's, Box VI was the girl's, Box VII was the boy's. My box was Box V." The novel is structured in four parts and composed not of chapters but of sections of various lengths, titled, for instance, ARCHIVE, DEPARTURE, FAMILY LEXICON, NARRATIVE ARC, ALONE TOGETHER, MAP, REVERBERATIONS, many of which are repeated numerous times throughout. Scattered among these are itemisations of the contents of each box: notebooks, maps, musical scores, books, compact discs, photographs and the like in Boxes I to V (which, as Luiselli states in an author's note, compose "[t]he fundamental 'bibliography'" of the text), as well as a transcription of echoes in Box VI, and Polaroid photographs in Box VII (which are collected by the girl and the boy during their journey). This itemisation is only one of the ways documentation and the composition of an archive are written into the novel. Elsewhere, in her own reflections as well as in her conversations with the children, the woman considers the purpose of keeping records, and worries over the uses to which those records might be put. Puzzling over his Polaroid camera, the boy asks:

> So what does it mean, Ma, to document stuff?
>
> Perhaps I should say that documenting is when you add thing plus light, light minus thing, photograph after photograph; or when you add sound, plus silence, minus sound, minus silence. What you have, in the end, are all the moments that didn't form part of the actual experience. ... Because experience, plus a

> document of the experience, is experience minus one. The strange thing is this: if, in the future one day, you add all those documents together again, what you have... is the experience. Or at least, a version of the experience that replaces the lived experience, even if what you originally documented were the moments cut out from it.

The woman struggles to formulate an appropriate answer, at first telling the boy that "[d]ocumenting just means to collect the present for posterity," then adding, simply, "I mean—for later." But, she realises, her definition isn't so simple after all, because matters are complicated by time:

> I'm not sure, though, what 'for later' means anymore. Something changed in the world. ... We feel time differently. ... And maybe the boy's frustration at not knowing what to take a picture of, or how to frame and focus the things he sees... is simply a sign of how our ways of documenting the world have fallen short. Perhaps if we found a new way to document it, we might begin to understand this new way we experience space and time. ... Finally, I tell the boy:
>
> You just have to find your own way of understanding space, so that the rest of us can feel less lost in time.

Time and space are interwoven here, and documentation becomes a kind of double helix via which—in retrospect—we can read a version of experience as it was lived in the so-called real world. But documents are not only made for later, or intended to be read solely in retrospect. Luiselli shows how the keeping of records and the composition of an archive also enable the discovery of an event in real time. "I suppose," the woman reflects, that "an archive gives you a kind of valley in which your thoughts can bounce back to you transformed. You whisper intuitions and thoughts into the emptiness, hoping to hear something back." Like Berger, looking from the life model to the empty space of the page before him, Luiselli whispers into the archive and listens for the echo, for the reverberations of the woman and the man and the boy and the girl, of Geronimo and the Eagle Warriors and the last free Apache, of child slaves, crusaders, and Orphan Train Riders, of unaccompanied and undocumented children, those who are found by Patrol Officers, but especially those who are lost, possibly forever. This novel is a working archive. It looks at the world directly: now, in the time and space of composition. And it documents this world for posterity. The story Luiselli seeks to understand—of the hemispheric war between North and South (which extends well beyond North and South America), of the fortification of borders between nations, within families, and separating the world from its representation—is continually unfolding, as it has been since at least the thirteenth century. There isn't time to wait to see how the story ends before beginning to tell it, as Luiselli has done with such virtuosity in *Lost Children Archive*, over and again, in many voices, from many angles.

XXXV

I STOPPED WALKING almost without noticing. Ali and I had just moved in together after a year and a half of living between my flat and his. We were in a new house, in a new neighbourhood. I was working three, sometimes four jobs, and learning (but more often struggling) to juggle work, a properly shared life, step-mothering and, in the gaps, writing. It was weeks after our move, maybe even months, before I noticed that I didn't know the names of the streets around our house and realised that, in most cases, I didn't even know where they led.

I know more now, more than three years later, but I still don't walk in the way I used to. I miss the river, along which I lived for so many years, and which fed my walks during that time. Here, the creeks have all been canalised. Even then, except when it floods, the water rarely runs. But I do have a garden and, from my desk, through the study window, I can mark the Virginia creeper's growth, note in it the shift from summer into autumn and, much later, into spring.

Thinking about it now, while I write it down, one of the things I've come to know is that when I stopped walking, I also stopped dreaming the world in a particular way: the way, perhaps, that Bachelard does, "dreaming by the river"—any river—in which flow the elemental memories of childhood. I have tried to right this loss by reading, by immersing myself in the world on the page and drawing connections between it and what I think I know of the world beyond. The essays in this book are so many outcomes of that reading practice. But another outcome is a question, one which has emerged in the process of gathering these essays together, of thinking on the connections between them, as well as the connections between the word and the world. When I stopped walking, when I lost that immediate physical connection between the word and the world, did I also lose that sensual proof of existence, the third dimension?

It's May 2019, and I'm still reading Ali Smith's *Spring*. I'm up to the part where Brittany and Florence are on a train to Edinburgh. Florence is telling Brit about the seventeenth century Dutchman who invented the microscope and about "the invisible life she says there is in *this*": a drop of water. (The world dreamed from water, again.) Brit's attention is dropping in and out, as it does, shifting between Florence and the other people in the train carriage and her own interior thoughts, but she does hear Florence say that "looking is just the start of understanding, just its surface, the top layer of any understanding," and because she hears it, so do we.

Looking is a way of seeing the world. But if by looking, we see and understand only the surface of things, then perhaps we need art—Berger's working drawings, say, or Luiselli's and Laing's living archives, or Kinsky's Polaroids, or Farmer's (via Matisse's) red fish, or Tacita Dean's found and reframed photographs (reframed again by Smith)—to sound the depths of the world beyond the surface of the page.

I need art in this way. In the same way, I now know, that I need to walk.

Notes on Sources

I.

This fragment draws upon the work of Iain Sinclair, in particular *Lights Out for the Territory: 9 Excursions in the Secret History of London* (Granta, 1997). I have also cited Virginia Woolf's essay 'Street Haunting: A London Adventure' from *The Crowded Dance of Modern Life* (Penguin, 1993) and Gaston Bachelard's *The Poetics of Reverie: Childhood, Language and the Cosmos* (trans. Daniel Russell, Beacon Press, 1971).

II-IV.

In addition to Esther Kinsky's *River* (trans. Iain Galbraith, Fitzcarraldo Editions, 2017), this essay draws upon the following sources: Henry David Thoreau's essay 'Walking' from *Wild Apples and Other Natural History Essays* (ed. William Rossi, University of Georgia Press, 2002); Iain Galbraith's 'Translator's Introduction' to W.G. Sebald's *Across the Land and the Water: Selected Poems, 1964-2001* (trans. Iain Galbraith, Hamish Hamilton, 2011); Iain Sinclair's *London Orbital: A Walk Around the M25* (Penguin, 2003); Gareth Rees' *Marshland: Dreams and Nightmares on the Edge of London* (Influx Press, 2013); Gaston Bachelard's *Water and Dreams: An Essay on the Imagination of Matter* (trans. Edith R. Farrell, Dallas Institute for Humanities & Culture, 1999); and Will Self's *Psychogeography* (Bloomsbury, 2007).

V.

This fragment is indebted to Kristin Otto's *Yarra: A Diverting History of Melbourne's Murky River* (Text, 2009).

VI.

This essay is a reading of Katharine Kilalea's *OK, Mr Field* (Faber and Faber, 2018).

VII.

In addition to Jorge Consiglio's *Southerly* (trans. Cherilyn Elston, Charco Press, 2017), the following sources are cited in this essay: Jorge Luis Borges' story 'The South', from his *Collected Fictions* (trans. Andrew Hurley, Penguin, 1998); Gaston Bachelard's *The Poetics of Space* (trans. Maria Jolas, Beacon Press, 1969); and Eva Hoffman's *Time* (Profile Books, 2009).

IX.

This fragment is indebted to Ali Smith's *Spring* (Hamish Hamilton, 2019).

X-XII.

This essay is a reading of the works of Olivia Laing: *To the River: A Journey Beneath the Surface* (Canongate, 2011); *The Trip to Echo Spring: Why Writers Drink* (Canongate, 2013); *The Lonely City: Adventures in the Art of Being Alone* (Canongate, 2016); and *Crudo: A Novel* (Picador, 2018). The Centre Pompidou exhibition I refer to is *Le Movement des Image* (2006). 'Intimacy' was shown at The Australian Centre for Contemporary Art in 2008.

XIII.

This fragment is indebted to Beverley Farmer's *A Body of Water* (University of Queensland Press, 1990).

XIV.

In addition to Fiona Wright's two collections of essays, *The World Was Whole* (Giramondo, 2018) and *Small Acts of Disappearance: Essays on Hunger* (Giramondo, 2015), this essay draws upon Gaston Bachelard's *The Poetics of Space* (trans. Maria Jolas, Beacon Press, 1969).

XV.

This fragment is indebted to Beverley Farmer's *Alone* (Sisters Publishing, 1980). It also cites J.L. Carr's *A Month in Country* (Penguin, 2000).

XVI-XXI.

Alongside Mariana Dimópulos' *All My Goodbyes* (trans. Alice Whitmore, Giramondo, 2017), this essay draws upon the following sources: Walter Benjamin's 'One-Way Street' from *Walter Benjamin: Selected Writings: Volume 1, 1913-1926* (trans. Edmund Jephcott, Belknap Press, 1996); Valeria Luiselli's 'Other Rooms' in *Sidewalks* (trans. Christina MacSweeney, Granta, 2013); Carlo Rovelli's *Seven Brief Lessons on Physics* (trans. Simon Carnell and Erica Segre, Penguin, 2016); Rebecca Solnit's *Wanderlust: A History of Walking* (Verso, 2001); and Susan Sontag's 'Under the Sign of Saturn' in *Under the Sign of Saturn* (Noonday Press, 1978).

XXII.

This fragment is particularly indebted to Deborah Levy's *The Cost of Living* (Hamish Hamilton, 2018).

XXIII.

In addition to Suneeta Peres da Costa's *Saudade* (Giramondo, 2018), the following works are cited in this essay: Valeria Luiselli's 'Alternative Routes' in *Sidewalks* (trans. Christina MacSweeney, Granta, 2013); Elizabeth Bishop's introduction to *An Anthology of Twentieth-Century Brazilian Poetry* (Wesleyan University Press, 1972); 'An Interview with Antonio Tabucchi' in *Contemporary Literature* (Autumn 1994); Nick Cave's 'The Secret Life of the Love Song' in *The Complete Lyrics* (Penguin, 2007); Fernando Pessoa's *The Book of Disquiet* (trans. Margaret Jull Costa, Serpent's Tail, 1991); and Simone Weil's 'Love' in *Gravity and Grace* (trans. Emma Crawford and Mario von der Ruhr, Routledge, 2002).

XXIV.

These fragments are inspired by reading Beverley Farmer's *A Body of Water* (University of Queensland Press, 1990); Deborah Levy's *The Cost of Living* (Hamish Hamilton, 2018); and Olivia Laing's *Crudo* (Picador, 2018).

XXV-XXVII.

This essay is a reading of four of Cynan Jones' novels: *The Long Dry* (Granta, 2006); Everything *I Found On the Beach* (Parthian, 2011); *The Dig* (Granta, 2014); and *Cove* (Granta, 2016).

XXVIII.

These fragments are inspired by reading Robert Macfarlane's *The Wild Places* (Granta, 2007); Meredith Hooper's *The Longest Winter* (John Murray, 2010); Records of the British National Antarctic Expedition, 1910-1913, held at the Scott Polar Research Institute at Cambridge, in particular the Journal kept by Victor L.A. Campbell from the landing of the Northern Party at Evans Cove, Victoria Land and during their sledge journey to Cape Evans, 8 January to

21 October 1912; and, always, the four prose narratives of W.G. Sebald, *Vertigo* (trans. Michael Hulse, Harvill Press, 2000), *The Emigrants* (trans. Michael Hulse, Vintage, 2002), *The Rings of Saturn* (trans. Michael Hulse, Vintage, 2002), and *Austerlitz* (trans. Anthea Bell, Penguin, 2001).

XXIX.

This is a reading of Samanta Schweblin's *Mouthful of Birds* (trans. Megan McDowell, OneWorld, 2019).

XXX.

This fragment cites Anita Brookner's *A Start in Life* (Penguin, 2017).

XXXI-XXXIV.

In addition to reading Valeria Luiselli's *Lost Children Archive* (4th Estate, 2019) and *Tell Me How it Ends: An Essay in Forty Questions* (Coffee House Press, 2017), this essay draws upon the following sources: Chloe Aridjis' *Asunder* (Vintage, 2014); John Berger's 'Drawing' from his *Selected Essays* (ed. Geoff Dyer, Bloomsbury, 2001); Teju Cole's *Blind Spot* (Faber and Faber, 2016); and W.G. Sebald's *The Emigrants* (trans. Michael Hulse, Vintage, 2002), *Vertigo* (trans. Michael Hulse, Harvill Press, 2000) and his interview with Michael Silverblatt published as 'A Poem of an Invisible Subject' in *The Emergence of Memory* (ed. Lynne Sharon Schwartz, Seven Stories Press, 2007).

XXXV.

This fragment returns to Ali Smith's *Spring* (Hamish Hamilton, 2019).

Acknowledgements

Many of the essays in this collection have been published previously in *3AM Magazine*, *Splice*, and *The Sydney Review of Books*. Thank you to the editors of these publications for their support and advice. In particular, thank you to Tristan Foster who first encouraged me to write extended review essays. Thanks, too, to Peter Rose and Amy Baillieu, who published my first work as a critic in the *Australian Book Review*.

Thank you to Daniel Davis Wood for so many things: for the opportunity to write for *Splice* in all its incarnations; for his tremendously generous support; and for his unparalleled acuity in reading, editing and generally overseeing the development of this collection.

Thank you to Rosy and Bill Morton of The Paperback Bookshop. The Paperback helped to make me the reader that I now am and I'm immensely grateful to be a part of it.

Special thanks go to my parents, Helen and Patrick MacDonald, who encouraged me to read even (or, especially) when I wanted to be out in the world instead. And to my partner, Ali Alizadeh, who encouraged me to write even (or, especially) when I complained that there was no time and no space, and no quiet to do it in. This book is for you.

SPLICE
ThisIsSplice.co.uk

www.ingramcontent.com/pod-product-compliance
Lightning Source LLC
Chambersburg PA
CBHW030639190726
48286CB00008B/2588

* 9 7 8 1 9 1 6 1 7 3 0 2 6 *